CODE ON THE CLOUD: AZURE FOR DEVELOPERS

FIRST EDITION

Preface

Welcome to the first edition of *Azure 101: The No-Fluff Beginner's Guide* — a comprehensive, hands-on introduction to cloud development with Microsoft Azure. This book was born from a desire to create an approachable yet technically sound resource for those taking their first steps into the world of cloud computing. Whether you're a student, a hobbyist, or a professional developer pivoting into cloud-native development, this book aims to provide clarity without overwhelming you with unnecessary jargon.

Cloud computing is no longer an optional skill; it's become the backbone of modern application development. As digital transformation accelerates across industries, developers need to understand how to leverage cloud platforms effectively. Azure, with its expansive suite of services and deep integration with the Microsoft ecosystem, is a compelling choice for developers at all levels.

This book is organized into nine chapters that progressively take you from foundational knowledge to advanced, real-world applications of Azure services. We start with the basics: what the cloud is, why Azure matters, and the core paradigms behind cloud development. We then walk through the process of setting up your development environment, exploring key services such as Azure App Services, Azure Functions, and databases tailored for the cloud.

As you progress, you'll learn how to build cloud-native applications using microservices and serverless architectures, how to secure your applications using tools like Azure Key Vault, and how to monitor and scale them effectively. The book also includes advanced use cases such as integrating AI and Kubernetes, along with practical scenarios like migrating legacy apps or building SaaS platforms.

In Chapter 7, we dive into real-world solutions and strategies, ensuring you're prepared to apply your skills in production settings. Chapter 8 focuses on growth — how to continue learning, engage with the community, and map your career path within the Azure ecosystem.

The appendices provide a wealth of additional resources, including a glossary of terms, sample projects, and frequently asked questions that new Azure developers often encounter.

The cloud landscape is vast and constantly evolving. This book won't make you an expert overnight, but it *will* give you the solid foundation you need to start building real solutions with Azure. We've cut through the noise to bring you practical insights and techniques, making it easier for you to start your cloud development journey with confidence.

Table of Contents

16 | Code On The Cloud

Chapter 1: Introduction to Cloud Development with Azure

The Evolution of Cloud Computing

Cloud computing has fundamentally transformed how software is developed, deployed, and maintained. It has changed not only the infrastructure of applications but also the way developers think about scalability, availability, and cost. Understanding its evolution provides the necessary context to appreciate why platforms like Microsoft Azure are pivotal in modern software development.

From Mainframes to Microservices

The journey to the cloud began decades ago with centralized mainframe computing. Organizations hosted applications on single, powerful machines accessed via thin clients. This model offered simplicity but limited scalability and flexibility.

As the internet grew, so did the complexity of computing needs. The industry shifted toward a client-server model, followed by distributed computing. This change allowed for better load distribution and resource utilization but introduced new challenges around maintenance, security, and cost.

The 2000s saw the rise of virtualization, enabling multiple virtual machines (VMs) to run on a single physical server. This was a game-changer—it improved hardware efficiency and paved the way for more flexible deployment models. Companies no longer needed to overprovision physical hardware; they could scale virtual resources based on demand.

From virtualization, the next logical step was cloud computing—offering computing resources (compute, storage, databases, networking) as on-demand services over the internet. The three key service models emerged:

- **Infrastructure as a Service (IaaS)**: Provisioning virtual machines and networking components.

- **Platform as a Service (PaaS)**: Providing a managed environment for developing and deploying applications.

- **Software as a Service (SaaS)**: Delivering complete software solutions via the web.

The Cloud Era: Why It Matters

In the cloud era, developers no longer need to worry about provisioning hardware, configuring networks, or maintaining servers. Instead, they focus on writing code and building features.

Benefits of the cloud model include:

- **Elastic scalability**: Resources can scale up or down automatically.

- **Pay-as-you-go pricing**: You pay only for what you use.

- **Global availability**: Applications can be deployed across data centers worldwide.

- **Rapid deployment**: Infrastructure can be provisioned in minutes.

- **Built-in resilience**: Cloud providers offer high availability, disaster recovery, and automated backups.

The Emergence of Azure

Microsoft Azure launched in 2010 as a cloud computing platform and has since evolved into one of the largest cloud ecosystems. Initially known as Windows Azure, the platform expanded far beyond Windows-based services and now supports a wide range of operating systems, frameworks, and programming languages.

Azure is currently used by startups, Fortune 500 companies, and government organizations. Its seamless integration with tools like Visual Studio, GitHub, and Microsoft 365 makes it especially appealing to developers already within the Microsoft ecosystem.

Some defining features of Azure include:

- A vast selection of services (over 200) spanning compute, storage, AI, DevOps, and more.

- Deep support for hybrid cloud and on-premises integrations.

- Enterprise-grade security and compliance.

- First-party tools for identity management (Azure AD), monitoring (Azure Monitor), and infrastructure-as-code (Bicep, ARM templates, Terraform support).

Cloud-Native Development: A Paradigm Shift

Cloud-native is more than a buzzword. It represents a fundamental shift in how applications are designed, developed, and operated. The goal is to build systems that are:

- **Resilient**: Able to handle failures gracefully.

- **Scalable**: Can grow or shrink based on demand.

- **Observable**: Provide insights into their health and performance.

- **Automated**: Deployed and managed via CI/CD pipelines and infrastructure-as-code.

- **Containerized**: Built using Docker and orchestrated with Kubernetes.

In this model, traditional monolithic applications give way to **microservices**—small, independently deployable services that work together. Serverless architectures, where developers write small units of code executed in response to events, further simplify operations.

Here's a basic example of a serverless Azure Function written in JavaScript:

```
module.exports = async function (context, req) {
    context.log('HTTP trigger function received a request.');

    const name = (req.query.name || (req.body && req.body.name));
    const responseMessage = name
        ? `Hello, ${name}. Welcome to Azure Functions!`
        : "This HTTP triggered function executed successfully. Pass
a name in the query string or in the request body.";

    context.res = {
        status: 200,
        body: responseMessage
    };
};
```

This function scales automatically, only runs when triggered (e.g., by an HTTP request), and incurs costs only when executed.

Cloud Skills: The Developer's Competitive Edge

As businesses adopt the cloud, developers who understand cloud-native patterns and services are in high demand. Companies are shifting away from on-prem infrastructure in favor of cloud platforms, not just for cost savings, but for the agility and innovation they enable.

Knowing how to:

- Deploy code using CI/CD pipelines

- Set up auto-scaling environments

- Build APIs that connect to cloud databases

- Implement security using identity providers like Azure AD

- Monitor applications using built-in observability tools

…makes you a valuable asset in any team.

The Role of DevOps and Automation

The DevOps movement has significantly influenced cloud development. Azure supports DevOps practices through:

- **Azure DevOps**: End-to-end toolchain for CI/CD, project management, and testing.

- **GitHub Actions**: Automating workflows directly within GitHub repositories.

- **Infrastructure as Code**: Using tools like Terraform or ARM templates to version and automate resource provisioning.

Example: a simple Azure CLI command to create a resource group:

```
az group create --name myResourceGroup --location eastus
```

Automation like this speeds up development and reduces the potential for human error.

Conclusion: A Foundation for What's Next

The evolution of cloud computing has reached a point where developers must embrace new tools, architectures, and workflows to stay relevant. Azure is at the forefront of this change, providing a rich and expanding ecosystem that supports a wide array of development scenarios.

As we move forward in this book, you'll gain practical experience with Azure services, learn how to build and deploy applications in the cloud, and explore real-world strategies for security, scaling, and automation. Whether you're aiming to build your first serverless app or architect an enterprise-grade SaaS product, the journey begins here — with a solid understanding of where cloud computing came from, and where it's heading.

Why Azure for Developers?

In a world filled with multiple cloud providers—Amazon Web Services (AWS), Google Cloud Platform (GCP), IBM Cloud, and others—it's natural to ask: *Why choose Microsoft Azure?* For developers, the answer lies not only in Azure's breadth of services but in how it empowers efficient, scalable, secure, and modern application development. Whether you're building a small prototype or architecting enterprise-grade systems, Azure provides a well-integrated, developer-friendly ecosystem that supports rapid innovation and growth.

A Mature and Expansive Cloud Platform

Microsoft Azure is the second-largest public cloud provider globally, with a presence in more than 60+ regions and over 200 data centers. It offers a vast array of services across domains such as computing, storage, databases, AI, analytics, IoT, and networking.

Azure's maturity means developers gain access to highly stable services, comprehensive documentation, robust support, and a thriving community. For example:

- Azure App Services streamline web app deployment with built-in scaling and SSL.

- Azure Functions enable serverless development, letting you run code without managing infrastructure.

- Azure Logic Apps allow you to visually design automated workflows that integrate with various systems.

Azure's diverse service catalog also means developers can find tools tailored to almost any use case—from game development to scientific research.

Integration with Microsoft Ecosystem

One of Azure's key advantages lies in its seamless integration with Microsoft products, which are deeply embedded in many enterprise environments. Developers working within the Microsoft stack (e.g., .NET, C#, Visual Studio, SQL Server) will find Azure to be the most natural choice.

Examples of integration include:

- **Azure Active Directory (Azure AD)** for single sign-on across Microsoft 365, SharePoint, and custom apps.

- **Azure DevOps** for managing source code, CI/CD pipelines, and agile project planning.

- **Visual Studio and Visual Studio Code** have built-in Azure tooling, making it easy to deploy apps, create resources, or debug cloud-hosted applications.

Even developers working in other languages like Python, Java, Node.js, or Go benefit from Azure's extensive SDKs and runtime support.

Here's a sample snippet using the Azure SDK for Python to upload a file to Azure Blob Storage:

```
from azure.storage.blob import BlobServiceClient
```

```
connect_str =
"DefaultEndpointsProtocol=https;AccountName=youraccount;AccountKey=y
ourkey;"
blob_service_client =
BlobServiceClient.from_connection_string(connect_str)

container_client = blob_service_client.get_container_client("my-
container")
with open("sample.txt", "rb") as data:
    container_client.upload_blob(name="sample.txt", data=data)
```

This SDK-first approach empowers developers to work in the languages they love without sacrificing capability.

Developer Experience and Tooling

Azure's developer tooling is among the best in the industry. Microsoft has invested heavily in making the developer experience seamless, productive, and customizable.

Key developer-focused features include:

- **Azure CLI**: A powerful cross-platform command-line interface for managing Azure resources.

- **Azure PowerShell**: Ideal for Windows-based automation and script-heavy tasks.

- **Azure SDKs**: Available for JavaScript/TypeScript, Python, .NET, Java, and more.

- **Bicep Language**: A declarative infrastructure-as-code (IaC) language native to Azure, simpler than JSON ARM templates.

Using the Azure CLI, developers can provision resources with a single line:

```
az webapp up --name myapp --resource-group my-rg --runtime "NODE|16-
lts"
```

This command creates a web app, provisions hosting, and deploys your code—all in one go.

Developers can also benefit from services like GitHub Copilot, GitHub Codespaces, and GitHub Actions—all of which integrate directly into Azure workflows.

End-to-End DevOps Support

From planning to deployment, Azure supports the full DevOps lifecycle. Developers can use tools like:

- **Azure Repos**: Host Git repositories.

- **Azure Pipelines**: Automate builds and releases.

- **Azure Test Plans**: Manage and execute manual and automated tests.

- **Azure Artifacts**: Host NuGet, npm, Maven, and Python packages.

Azure also integrates natively with **GitHub**, allowing developers to use GitHub Actions for continuous deployment. Here's a sample GitHub Actions YAML file that deploys an app to Azure App Service:

```yaml
name: Deploy to Azure

on:
  push:
    branches:
      - main

jobs:
  build-and-deploy:
    runs-on: ubuntu-latest
    steps:
      - uses: actions/checkout@v2

      - name: Set up Node.js
        uses: actions/setup-node@v2
        with:
          node-version: '16'

      - run: npm install
      - run: npm run build

      - name: Deploy to Azure Web App
        uses: azure/webapps-deploy@v2
        with:
          app-name: 'myapp'
          slot-name: 'production'
          publish-profile: ${{ secrets.AZURE_WEBAPP_PUBLISH_PROFILE
}}
```

```
package: '.'
```

Azure enables you to treat infrastructure as code, integrate testing in your pipeline, and manage releases—all in one unified flow.

Security and Compliance for Enterprise-Grade Apps

Security is a cornerstone of Azure's offering. Developers building applications that handle sensitive data benefit from Microsoft's enterprise-level security, compliance, and governance features.

Notable services include:

- **Azure Key Vault**: Securely manage secrets, keys, and certificates.

- **Azure Defender**: Threat protection across workloads.

- **Microsoft Entra (Azure AD)**: Identity management and conditional access policies.

- **Policy and Blueprints**: Enforce resource configurations and governance rules.

A sample Key Vault access code in C#:

```
var kvUri = "https://<your-key-vault-name>.vault.azure.net/";
var client = new SecretClient(new Uri(kvUri), new
DefaultAzureCredential());

KeyVaultSecret secret = await
client.GetSecretAsync("DbConnectionString");
string connectionString = secret.Value;
```

Azure also meets rigorous compliance standards such as ISO, HIPAA, GDPR, FedRAMP, and SOC, making it suitable for sectors like finance, healthcare, and government.

Hybrid and Multicloud Capabilities

Azure's leadership in **hybrid cloud** is unmatched, thanks to solutions like:

- **Azure Arc**: Manage resources across on-premises, other clouds, and edge environments.

- **Azure Stack**: Extend Azure services into your datacenter.

- **Azure Site Recovery**: Enable business continuity with failover to the cloud.

Developers can build apps that span cloud and on-prem infrastructure seamlessly, making Azure a great fit for companies with legacy systems that can't be fully migrated yet.

Moreover, with **Azure API Management**, **Event Grid**, and **Service Bus**, developers can build integrations across platforms and technologies effortlessly.

AI, Data, and Analytics Services

Azure isn't just for hosting applications—it's also a leader in AI and data services. Developers can easily enhance their apps with intelligent features using:

- **Azure Cognitive Services**: Add vision, speech, language, and decision capabilities.

- **Azure OpenAI Service**: Integrate models like GPT for advanced NLP tasks.

- **Azure Machine Learning**: Build, train, and deploy machine learning models at scale.

Sample integration of Azure OpenAI with a Node.js app:

```
const { OpenAIClient, AzureKeyCredential } =
require("@azure/openai");

const endpoint = "https://<your-openai-resource>.openai.azure.com/";
const apiKey = "<your-api-key>";
const client = new OpenAIClient(endpoint, new
AzureKeyCredential(apiKey));

const response = await client.getCompletions("deployment-id", {
    prompt: "List five cloud computing benefits",
    maxTokens: 50
});
console.log(response.choices[0].text);
```

For data-intensive apps, Azure also offers:

- **Azure Synapse Analytics**: Unified big data and data warehousing.

- **Azure Data Factory**: ETL pipelines and data transformation.

- **Azure Cosmos DB**: Globally distributed NoSQL database.

These tools allow developers to create real-time, AI-enhanced, data-rich applications with ease.

Community, Learning, and Support

Azure's ecosystem is developer-friendly not just in tooling but also in community and learning resources. Microsoft provides:

- **Microsoft Learn**: Free interactive tutorials and labs.

- **Docs and Quickstarts**: Exhaustive official documentation with code samples.

- **Azure Friday**: Weekly video series from Microsoft engineers.

- **GitHub Sample Projects**: Open source templates and examples.

There are also global events like **Microsoft Build**, **Ignite**, and regional meetups that foster community learning and collaboration. Additionally, developers can earn **Microsoft Certifications** to validate their skills and stand out in the job market.

Summary: Azure Empowers Developers

Azure offers a unified platform for developers that supports modern cloud-native patterns, multiple programming languages, robust tooling, end-to-end DevOps, and seamless scalability. It allows developers to focus on writing innovative applications, not managing infrastructure.

By choosing Azure, developers gain access to:

- A mature, scalable cloud platform

- Rich SDKs and automation tools

- Seamless integration with Microsoft services

- First-class DevOps and CI/CD support

- Security and compliance for enterprise apps

- Broad AI and data capabilities

- A supportive and growing community

Azure isn't just another cloud—it's a developer-first platform built for building the future of software. Whether you're creating a simple web app, a complex microservices architecture, or a machine-learning-powered API, Azure provides the foundation, tools, and support you need to succeed.

Key Concepts and Terminology

Before diving deeper into Azure development, it's critical to grasp the foundational concepts and terminology that underpin cloud computing. Understanding these concepts will ensure you can follow best practices, make informed architectural decisions, and confidently interact with the Azure ecosystem. This section unpacks the key ideas, models, and language that every Azure developer must be fluent in.

The Cloud Service Models

Cloud computing is typically divided into three primary service models. Understanding their differences is vital for selecting the right tools for your application:

- **Infrastructure as a Service (IaaS)**
  This model offers virtualized computing resources over the internet. Developers get access to virtual machines (VMs), storage, and networking but are responsible for managing the OS, middleware, and runtime.
  Example: Azure Virtual Machines

- **Platform as a Service (PaaS)**
  PaaS provides a managed environment where developers can build, deploy, and scale applications without worrying about the underlying infrastructure.
  Example: Azure App Service, Azure Functions

- **Software as a Service (SaaS)**
  SaaS delivers fully functional applications over the internet, eliminating the need for installation or maintenance.
  Example: Microsoft 365, Outlook.com

Cloud Deployment Models

Azure supports multiple deployment models, each suited to different business requirements and technical constraints:

- **Public Cloud**: All infrastructure and services are hosted on Azure's public infrastructure and shared across tenants.

- **Private Cloud**: Dedicated infrastructure hosted either on-prem or in a private datacenter.

- **Hybrid Cloud**: A mix of public and private cloud, allowing data and applications to be shared between them.

- **Multicloud**: Usage of multiple cloud providers (e.g., Azure + AWS) for redundancy or flexibility.

Azure enables hybrid and multicloud setups through services like **Azure Arc**, **Azure Stack**, and **ExpressRoute**, allowing on-premises and cloud resources to work in tandem.

Azure Resource Manager (ARM)

At the core of Azure's provisioning engine is **Azure Resource Manager (ARM)**—the deployment and management service for Azure. Everything in Azure, from VMs to databases, is considered a **resource**, and ARM provides a consistent management layer for:

- Creating and configuring resources

- Applying policies and role-based access control

- Managing deployments as atomic groups

ARM uses **Resource Groups** to organize related resources. For instance, an app, its database, and associated storage can be grouped for easier deployment and access control.

Here's an example ARM template snippet for deploying a simple web app:

```
{
  "$schema": "https://schema.management.azure.com/schemas/2019-04-01/deploymentTemplate.json#",
  "contentVersion": "1.0.0.0",
  "resources": [
    {
      "type": "Microsoft.Web/sites",
      "apiVersion": "2021-02-01",
      "name": "myWebApp",
      "location": "East US",
      "properties": {
        "serverFarmId": "myAppServicePlan"
      }
    }
  ]
}
```

ARM templates can be used in CI/CD pipelines and support parameterization for flexibility.

Key Azure Constructs

Azure's environment is structured into a hierarchy of management layers. Here are some essential constructs:

- **Tenant**: An instance of Azure Active Directory tied to an organization. It provides identity and access management.

- **Subscription**: A logical container used to provision resources. It associates resources with billing and quotas.

- **Resource Group**: A container for managing resources that share the same lifecycle or purpose.

- **Resource**: An individual Azure service (VM, database, app service, etc.).

- **Region**: A geographic location where Azure data centers reside. Example: East US, West Europe.

- **Availability Zone**: A physically separate zone within a region, providing high availability.

- **Service Principal**: An identity used by apps or automation tools to authenticate against Azure services.

Azure Identity and Access Management (IAM)

IAM in Azure is handled by **Azure Active Directory (Azure AD)**. Azure AD provides:

- **Users and Groups**: For organizing people within your organization.

- **Roles**: Define permissions (read, write, manage) using **Role-Based Access Control (RBAC)**.

- **Managed Identities**: Used to securely authenticate applications with Azure services without storing credentials.

RBAC Example using Azure CLI:

```
az role assignment create --assignee <user-email> --role
"Contributor" --scope /subscriptions/<subscription-
id>/resourceGroups/<resource-group-name>
```

Azure AD also supports authentication protocols like OAuth2.0, OpenID Connect, and SAML, enabling single sign-on (SSO) and secure API access.

Storage Types in Azure

Azure offers various storage options suited for different use cases:

- **Blob Storage**: Unstructured object storage for files, images, and backups.

- **Table Storage**: A NoSQL key-value store for semi-structured data.

- **Queue Storage**: Message queuing for distributed systems.

- **File Storage**: SMB-compliant shared file storage.

- **Disk Storage**: Persistent storage for Azure VMs.

Blob Storage Example using Azure CLI:

```
az storage blob upload --account-name mystorageaccount --container-
name mycontainer --name image.png --file ./image.png
```

Each storage type provides different tiers (Hot, Cool, Archive) for optimizing cost and performance.

Networking Concepts

Azure's virtual networking lets developers securely connect Azure resources to each other and to the internet. Key networking terms include:

- **Virtual Network (VNet)**: A logically isolated section of the Azure network.

- **Subnet**: A segment within a VNet.

- **Network Security Group (NSG)**: Firewall rules to allow or deny traffic.

- **Public IP/Private IP**: Used for exposing services to the internet or within the VNet.

- **Load Balancer**: Distributes traffic across multiple services or instances.

- **Application Gateway**: Provides HTTP load balancing and Web Application Firewall (WAF).

Sample NSG rule via CLI:

```
az network nsg rule create \
  --resource-group myRG \
  --nsg-name myNSG \
  --name allowSSH \
  --protocol tcp \
  --priority 1000 \
```

```
--destination-port-range 22 \
--access allow \
--direction inbound
```

Networking services in Azure are deeply customizable and scalable, supporting VPNs, ExpressRoute, and DNS zones.

Compute Services

Compute is at the heart of cloud development. Azure offers several compute models:

- **Azure Virtual Machines (VMs)**: Full control over the OS and environment.

- **Azure App Service**: PaaS model for hosting web and API applications.

- **Azure Functions**: Serverless compute that runs code in response to events.

- **Azure Kubernetes Service (AKS)**: Managed Kubernetes for containerized workloads.

- **Azure Container Instances (ACI)**: Quick container deployments without orchestration overhead.

Example of creating an Azure Function via CLI:

```
az functionapp create \
  --resource-group myResourceGroup \
  --consumption-plan-location westus \
  --runtime node \
  --functions-version 4 \
  --name myFunctionApp \
  --storage-account myStorageAccount
```

Monitoring and Observability

Azure provides comprehensive observability tools to monitor the health, usage, and performance of your applications:

- **Azure Monitor**: Collects logs, metrics, and diagnostics data.

- **Application Insights**: Provides performance and usage analytics for applications.

- **Log Analytics**: Query and analyze log data using Kusto Query Language (KQL).

Sample KQL query:

```
requests
| where timestamp > ago(1h)
| summarize count() by resultCode
```

These tools are critical for understanding how your app behaves in production and responding to issues proactively.

Developer Automation and Infrastructure as Code (IaC)

Azure strongly supports automation through:

- **ARM Templates** and **Bicep**

- **Terraform**: Open-source IaC tool with Azure provider support

- **Pulumi**: Code-first infrastructure management using general-purpose languages

Sample Bicep code to create a storage account:

```
resource storage 'Microsoft.Storage/storageAccounts@2022-05-01' = {
  name: 'mystorageacct'
  location: 'eastus'
  sku: {
    name: 'Standard_LRS'
  }
  kind: 'StorageV2'
  properties: {}
}
```

By embracing IaC, developers can version control their infrastructure, automate deployments, and enforce consistency.

Marketplace and APIs

Azure also includes:

- **Azure Marketplace**: Offers pre-configured virtual machines, app templates, APIs, and third-party services.

- **REST APIs and SDKs**: Nearly every Azure service is accessible via REST, with SDKs provided for common languages.

Sample API request using cURL:

```
curl -X GET
https://management.azure.com/subscriptions/{subscriptionId}/resource
s?api-version=2021-04-01 \
  -H "Authorization: Bearer <access_token>"
```

Knowing how to use the APIs opens the door to advanced automation and integrations.

Conclusion

The cloud introduces a vast array of services and capabilities. As an Azure developer, understanding the foundational terminology and architecture enables you to make the most of the platform. From compute and storage to identity, networking, and DevOps, each concept plays a role in delivering robust, scalable applications.

As we progress in this book, we'll build upon these concepts with practical examples and real-world implementations, helping you grow from familiarity to fluency in the Azure ecosystem.

Development Paradigms in the Cloud Era

As cloud computing has evolved, so too have the paradigms developers use to design, build, and deploy applications. In the on-premises world, developers were constrained by infrastructure, hardware procurement timelines, and manual configuration. But the cloud has removed many of those barriers, introducing a set of development paradigms that emphasize scalability, resilience, automation, and continuous delivery.

This section explores the dominant development paradigms in the cloud era—what they are, why they matter, and how they transform the way developers approach software creation.

The Shift from Monoliths to Microservices

One of the most important transitions in cloud-native development is the move from **monolithic** architectures to **microservices**.

Monolithic Architecture

A monolithic application is built as a single, indivisible unit. All components—UI, business logic, data access—are tightly coupled and deployed together. This model was simple to develop initially but becomes complex and fragile as the application grows.

Issues with monoliths in a cloud context:

- Difficult to scale individual components independently

- Longer deployment cycles

- Increased risk of regression from changes in a shared codebase

- Bottlenecks in team collaboration

Microservices Architecture

In contrast, a **microservices** approach decomposes an application into loosely coupled, independently deployable services. Each microservice encapsulates a specific business capability and communicates with others via APIs or messaging systems.

Benefits:

- Services can be scaled individually based on demand

- Teams can develop, test, and deploy services independently

- Easier adoption of diverse technologies (e.g., a Python service next to a Node.js service)

- Resilience and fault isolation

For example, an e-commerce system might have services for:

- User management

- Product catalog

- Order processing

- Payment handling

These services can be deployed across containers using Azure Kubernetes Service (AKS) or independently hosted on Azure App Service or Azure Functions.

Serverless Computing

Serverless is a paradigm where developers write small, stateless functions that are triggered by events. Azure Functions exemplify this model.

Key Characteristics:

- No server management

- Automatic scaling

- Event-driven execution

- Consumption-based pricing (pay only when code runs)

Common triggers include:

- HTTP requests

- Queue messages

- Blob uploads

- Timer schedules

Example: A function that resizes images when they're uploaded to Azure Blob Storage.

```
module.exports = async function (context, myBlob) {
    context.log("Processing blob: ", context.bindingData.name);
    // Image resizing logic here...
};
```

Serverless is ideal for lightweight, asynchronous tasks such as:

- Data ingestion

- Notification systems

- Background jobs

- API backends

However, it's not suitable for long-running or stateful workloads unless paired with tools like **Durable Functions**.

Event-Driven Architectures

Event-driven architecture (EDA) is a design paradigm in which components react to events rather than directly invoking one another. It decouples producers from consumers, increasing flexibility and scalability.

Components include:

- **Event producers**: Emit events (e.g., user registered)

- **Event consumers**: Subscribe to and react to events

- **Event broker**: Routes messages (e.g., Azure Event Grid, Azure Service Bus)

Example use case: When a new order is placed:

1. The Order service emits an event

2. Inventory service updates stock

3. Notification service sends a confirmation email

This enables:

- Loose coupling

- Asynchronous processing

- Scalability and parallelism

Azure services that support EDA:

- **Event Grid**: Lightweight publish-subscribe for events

- **Service Bus**: Reliable message queuing and topics

- **Event Hubs**: Telemetry ingestion at massive scale

DevOps and Continuous Delivery

In the cloud era, **DevOps** is not optional—it's foundational. DevOps combines development and operations practices to shorten the systems development lifecycle and ensure high software quality through automation.

Key DevOps practices:

- **CI/CD pipelines**: Automate build, test, and deployment

- **Infrastructure as Code (IaC)**: Manage infrastructure using declarative code

- **Monitoring and feedback loops**: Observe apps in real-time and adapt

Azure tooling includes:

- **Azure DevOps**: Pipelines, Repos, Artifacts, Boards

- **GitHub Actions**: Workflow automation from your GitHub repo

- **Terraform and Bicep**: Define infrastructure with code

- **Application Insights**: App monitoring and telemetry

Sample Azure Pipeline YAML:

```
trigger:
  branches:
    include:
      - main

jobs:
  - job: BuildDeploy
    pool:
      vmImage: 'ubuntu-latest'
    steps:
      - task: UseNode@2
        inputs:
          version: '18.x'
      - script: npm install && npm run build
        displayName: 'Install and Build'
      - task: AzureWebApp@1
        inputs:
          azureSubscription: '<connection-name>'
          appName: '<your-app-name>'
          package: '$(System.DefaultWorkingDirectory)/build'
```

These practices promote speed, reliability, and traceability in software delivery.

API-First and Headless Development

Another shift in modern development is **API-first** thinking, where APIs are not an afterthought but a primary concern. APIs define contracts between services, frontends, and clients.

Benefits:

- Enables frontend and backend to work in parallel

- Supports headless architectures (e.g., CMS decoupled from frontend)

- Facilitates reuse across mobile, web, IoT, etc.

Azure offers tools like:

- **Azure API Management**: Secure and monitor APIs

- **OpenAPI/Swagger support**: Auto-generate docs and clients

- **Logic Apps**: Compose APIs and workflows visually

API-first design is crucial for microservices, mobile apps, and composable enterprise architectures.

Containerization and Orchestration

Containers have become the standard for packaging applications. They encapsulate code, dependencies, and configuration, ensuring consistent behavior across environments.

Benefits of containers:

- Portability

- Rapid scaling

- Isolation

- Simplified testing

Azure supports:

- **Azure Container Instances (ACI)**: Run single containers quickly

- **Azure Kubernetes Service (AKS)**: Full-fledged container orchestration

- **Azure Container Registry (ACR)**: Host private Docker images

Sample Dockerfile for a Node.js app:

```
FROM node:18
WORKDIR /app
COPY . .
```

```
RUN npm install
CMD ["npm", "start"]
```

Kubernetes, with tools like Helm and Kustomize, supports complex workloads with advanced scheduling, autoscaling, and self-healing.

Infrastructure as Code (IaC)

IaC is a paradigm where infrastructure is provisioned using code rather than manual steps. This makes environments reproducible, version-controlled, and automatable.

Azure supports:

- **ARM Templates**: JSON-based IaC format

- **Bicep**: A simpler DSL for ARM

- **Terraform**: Cross-platform IaC tool

- **Pulumi**: Use general-purpose languages like TypeScript or Python for IaC

Benefits of IaC:

- Predictable and repeatable environments

- Easy rollback

- CI/CD integration

- Collaboration via version control

Example Bicep snippet:

```
resource storage 'Microsoft.Storage/storageAccounts@2022-05-01' = {
  name: 'myuniquestorage'
  location: 'eastus'
  sku: {
    name: 'Standard_LRS'
  }
  kind: 'StorageV2'
  properties: {}
}
```

This paradigm is foundational to modern DevOps.

Observability and Resilience

In cloud-native development, failures are inevitable. Rather than trying to prevent every error, modern systems are designed to withstand and recover from them gracefully.

Key resilience strategies:

- **Retries with backoff**

- **Circuit breakers**

- **Health checks**

- **Load balancing**

- **Graceful degradation**

Azure supports these through:

- **Application Gateway + WAF**

- **Azure Monitor and Alerts**

- **Azure Load Balancer**

- **Availability Zones and Auto-scaling**

Observability tools like **Application Insights**, **Log Analytics**, and **Distributed Tracing** help developers understand system behavior in production.

Feature Flags and Progressive Delivery

Releasing software in stages is safer than deploying everything at once. **Feature flags** and **progressive delivery** strategies (e.g., canary releases, blue-green deployments) enable this.

Azure Feature Management (via App Configuration) allows developers to toggle features without redeploying.

Example usage in .NET:

```
if (_featureManager.IsEnabledAsync("BetaFeature").Result)
{
    // Run new code
```

}

This practice reduces risk, improves velocity, and allows for targeted experimentation.

Summary

The cloud era has ushered in a revolution in software development. The dominant paradigms—microservices, serverless, DevOps, API-first, containers, and IaC—are transforming how applications are built, deployed, and operated. Azure provides a full ecosystem to support these paradigms with services that are scalable, secure, and developer-friendly.

Mastering these paradigms is not just about learning new tools—it's about embracing a mindset that values agility, automation, and resilience. As you build your skills on Azure, these paradigms will become second nature, empowering you to build robust, future-proof cloud-native applications.

Chapter 2: Setting Up for Azure Development

Creating and Configuring an Azure Account

Before you can begin building applications with Microsoft Azure, you need an active Azure account. Setting up your account is more than just registration—it's about configuring it for security, organization, cost control, and development workflows. This section will guide you through creating a new Azure account, setting up subscriptions and tenants, managing billing, applying best practices for access control, and preparing your account for development work.

Creating a Free Azure Account

Microsoft offers a generous **Azure free tier**, which is ideal for developers who are new to the platform. It includes:

- 12 months of popular services (e.g., Azure VMs, SQL Database, Blob Storage)

- 25+ services always free

- $200 USD Azure credit for the first 30 days

Steps to Create Your Account

1. Visit: https://azure.microsoft.com/free

2. Click **Start free**.

3. Sign in with an existing Microsoft account or create a new one.

4. Provide identity verification (phone and credit card).

5. Accept the terms and conditions.

6. Your free account and subscription are created automatically.

Understanding Tenants, Subscriptions, and Resource Groups

Once your account is ready, it's essential to understand Azure's logical structure.

Azure AD Tenant

An **Azure Active Directory (Azure AD) tenant** is the dedicated instance of Azure AD that your account belongs to. It handles identity management and access across your Azure resources. It includes:

- Users and groups

- App registrations

- Enterprise applications

Azure Subscription

An **Azure subscription** is the billing unit and container for resources. Each subscription can host multiple resource groups and services.

- A single tenant can have multiple subscriptions.

- You can use subscriptions to separate dev/test from production or isolate billing.

You can view your subscriptions using the Azure CLI:

```
az account list --output table
```

Resource Group

A **resource group** is a container for managing related Azure resources. All resources in a group share the same lifecycle and can be managed together.

Create a resource group using the CLI:

```
az group create --name MyResourceGroup --location eastus
```

Access Control and Security Best Practices

Setting up secure access is critical. Azure uses **Role-Based Access Control (RBAC)** to manage permissions.

Assigning Roles

Use built-in roles like:

- **Owner**: Full access

- **Contributor**: Can manage resources, but not access control

- **Reader**: View-only access

To assign a role:

```
az role assignment create \
  --assignee user@example.com \
  --role Contributor \
  --scope /subscriptions/<subscription-
id>/resourceGroups/MyResourceGroup
```

Using Azure AD Groups

Assigning permissions to **Azure AD groups** instead of individual users makes access easier to manage. Create a group via the Azure Portal or CLI, then assign roles at the group level.

Enabling Multi-Factor Authentication (MFA)

To secure admin accounts, enable MFA:

1. Go to Azure AD > Users > Multi-Factor Authentication.

2. Enforce MFA per user or via Conditional Access policies.

MFA helps prevent unauthorized access, especially for privileged accounts.

Managing Billing and Budgets

Cloud costs can grow unexpectedly if not monitored. Azure offers several tools to control and forecast spending.

Cost Management + Billing

Navigate to **Cost Management + Billing** in the Azure Portal to:

- View cost by resource group, service, or tag

- Forecast upcoming charges

- Set cost alerts

Creating Budgets

Set budgets to receive alerts when spending exceeds thresholds.

1. Go to Subscriptions > Select your subscription > Budgets.

2. Create a new budget with the desired amount.

3. Set up email alerts or integrate with Action Groups.

You can also tag resources for billing analysis:

```
az tag create --resource-id
/subscriptions/.../resourceGroups/MyResourceGroup --tags
environment=dev owner=frahaan
```

Tags help group and track resource spending effectively.

Setting Up Dev/Test and Production Environments

A well-structured account setup separates development and production workloads to avoid accidental disruptions or cost spikes.

Strategies:

*   **Separate Subscriptions**: Create a "Dev/Test" subscription and a "Production" subscription.

*   **Use Resource Groups**: Group resources logically by environment.

*   **Apply Naming Conventions**: Use prefixes or suffixes like -dev, -test, or -prod.

Example naming pattern:

*   `vm-web-dev`

*   `sql-orders-prod`

*   `storage-archive-test`

Consistent naming improves discoverability, governance, and automation.

Enabling and Managing Azure Policies

Azure **Policies** enforce rules on how resources can be created and used. This is helpful to ensure compliance, control costs, and standardize deployments.

Common Policies:

- Restrict locations to avoid costly regions

- Allow only specific VM sizes

- Enforce tags on resource creation

- Require disk encryption

Apply a built-in policy with CLI:

```
az policy assignment create \
  --name "enforce-tag" \
  --policy
"/providers/Microsoft.Authorization/policyDefinitions/require-tag" \
  --params '{"tagName":{"value":"owner"}}' \
  --scope /subscriptions/<subscription-
id>/resourceGroups/MyResourceGroup
```

Configuring Azure Portal and Dashboards

The **Azure Portal** is the web-based GUI for managing your resources.

Customizing the Portal

- **Pin resources to the dashboard** for quick access

- **Create dashboards** for teams or roles (e.g., dev dashboard, monitoring dashboard)

- Add **tiles** for metrics, resource statuses, alerts, and cost views

You can share dashboards with other users or groups.

Setting Up Azure CLI and Cloud Shell

The **Azure CLI** is a cross-platform tool for managing Azure from the command line.

Install CLI on your local machine:

- Windows: Use MSI installer

- macOS: Use Homebrew (`brew install azure-cli`)

- Linux: Use apt or yum

Login via:

```
az login
```

For browserless environments, use:

```
az login --use-device-code
```

Azure also offers **Cloud Shell**—a browser-based shell available directly from the Azure Portal. It provides pre-installed tools like Azure CLI, PowerShell, Git, Terraform, and Python.

Setting Up a Service Principal for Automation

To automate deployments (e.g., with CI/CD), create a **service principal**—an Azure AD identity for apps or scripts.

```
az ad sp create-for-rbac --name myApp --role Contributor --scopes
/subscriptions/<sub-id>
```

It returns credentials that can be stored securely in GitHub Secrets, Azure Key Vault, or CI/CD systems like Azure Pipelines.

Installing and Connecting Development Tools

To prepare for development, install these tools:

- **Visual Studio Code** (VS Code): Lightweight, extensible editor

- **Azure Extensions for VS Code**: Azure Account, Functions, App Service, Bicep, Terraform

- **Azure CLI / PowerShell**: For automation

- **Git**: Version control

In VS Code, sign in to Azure via the Azure extension, then browse and manage resources directly from the editor.

You can also deploy from VS Code using the Azure App Service extension:

1. Right-click your project folder.

2. Click "Deploy to Web App."

3. Select your subscription and resource.

Summary and Best Practices

Setting up your Azure account properly lays the groundwork for scalable, secure, and efficient cloud development. Key steps include:

- Creating a free Azure account

- Understanding tenants, subscriptions, and resource groups

- Applying RBAC for access control

- Managing billing and cost alerts

- Structuring environments for Dev/Test/Prod

- Using policies to enforce governance

- Installing CLI tools and extensions for productivity

By configuring your account with security and scalability in mind, you ensure that future development activities are smooth, compliant, and cost-effective. In the next section, we'll explore Azure CLI and PowerShell—two essential tools for managing Azure like a pro.

Azure CLI and PowerShell Essentials

When working with Azure, one of the most powerful tools you can use for managing resources and automating tasks is the **Azure Command-Line Interface (CLI)** and **PowerShell**. Both tools offer robust capabilities for interacting with Azure, and knowing how to use them efficiently can significantly boost your productivity and streamline your workflow.

This section will cover the essentials of Azure CLI and PowerShell, highlighting the key commands, workflows, and best practices you need to know in order to work with Azure efficiently.

Introduction to Azure CLI

The **Azure CLI** is a cross-platform command-line tool designed for managing Azure resources. It is available on Windows, macOS, and Linux, and it allows you to perform a wide range of tasks without needing to navigate the Azure Portal. Azure CLI is particularly well-suited for developers, system administrators, and automation tasks, as it provides easy-to-use commands for managing everything from virtual machines to networking and databases.

Installing Azure CLI

Before you can start using the Azure CLI, you need to install it. Here's how to do it on various operating systems:

- **Windows**: You can install Azure CLI via the MSI installer or by using **Windows Package Manager** (`winget install Microsoft.AzureCLI`).

- **macOS**: Install via **Homebrew**: `brew install azure-cli`.

- **Linux**: Installation steps vary depending on the distribution, but the easiest method is to follow the instructions on the Azure CLI installation page.

Once installed, you can verify the installation by running the following command in your terminal:

```
az --version
```

This will display the installed version of the Azure CLI, confirming that it is set up correctly.

Logging In to Azure CLI

To interact with Azure resources, you need to authenticate yourself. Use the following command to log in:

```
az login
```

This will open a browser window asking you to authenticate with your Azure account. If you're working in a headless environment, you can use the `--use-device-code` flag to log in using a code on another device.

```
az login --use-device-code
```

After successful login, you can verify your account and subscription with:

```
az account show
```

This will display information about your current subscription, including the subscription ID and tenant ID.

Common Azure CLI Commands

Once logged in, you can start working with Azure resources. Here are some essential commands:

Creating a Resource Group: A resource group is a logical container for your Azure resources. To create one, use:

```
az group create --name myResourceGroup --location eastus
```

-

Listing Resources: You can list all resources in a resource group using:

```
az resource list --resource-group myResourceGroup
```

-

Creating a Virtual Machine: To create a virtual machine, you can use:

```
az vm create --resource-group myResourceGroup --name myVM --image
UbuntuLTS --admin-username azureuser --generate-ssh-keys
```

- This command will create a new virtual machine in the specified resource group using the Ubuntu LTS image.

Managing Storage: You can create a storage account with:

```
az storage account create --name mystorageaccount --resource-group
myResourceGroup --sku Standard_LRS --location eastus
```

-

Scaling Virtual Machines: To scale a VM instance (e.g., changing the size), use:

```
az vm resize --resource-group myResourceGroup --name myVM --size
Standard_DS3_v2
```

-

Working with Resource Groups

Resource groups are a fundamental unit of management in Azure. They allow you to manage resources collectively. Here's how you can work with resource groups:

Listing Resource Groups:

```
az group list --output table
```

-

Deleting a Resource Group: Deleting a resource group will remove all resources inside it.

```
az group delete --name myResourceGroup --yes --no-wait
```

-

Scripting with Azure CLI

One of the powerful features of Azure CLI is the ability to automate tasks using scripts. You can save your commands in a shell script or batch file, which can be executed multiple times. Here's a simple example of creating a VM and a storage account using a script:

```bash
#!/bin/bash

# Set variables
resourceGroup="myResourceGroup"
location="eastus"
vmName="myVM"
storageAccount="mystorageaccount"

# Create resource group
az group create --name $resourceGroup --location $location

# Create storage account
az storage account create --name $storageAccount --resource-group $resourceGroup --sku Standard_LRS --location $location

# Create virtual machine
az vm create --resource-group $resourceGroup --name $vmName --image UbuntuLTS --admin-username azureuser --generate-ssh-keys
```

Introduction to Azure PowerShell

Azure PowerShell is another powerful tool for managing Azure resources, but it's designed specifically for Windows environments and the PowerShell scripting language. PowerShell is a task automation framework, and its syntax is built for system administrators and automation tasks.

PowerShell is a great option if you are familiar with the Windows environment or prefer working in a command shell with more advanced scripting capabilities than the Azure CLI.

Installing Azure PowerShell

To install Azure PowerShell, follow these steps:

Windows: You can install the latest version of Azure PowerShell from the PowerShell Gallery by running:

```
Install-Module -Name Az -AllowClobber -Force -Scope CurrentUser
```

-
- **macOS/Linux**: For macOS and Linux, use the platform-specific installation instructions provided by Microsoft on this page.

Logging In to Azure PowerShell

After installation, you can log in to Azure PowerShell using:

```
Connect-AzAccount
```

This command will prompt you to authenticate through a browser.

Common Azure PowerShell Commands
Creating a Resource Group:

```
New-AzResourceGroup -Name myResourceGroup -Location eastus
```

-

Listing Resources:

```
Get-AzResource -ResourceGroupName myResourceGroup
```

-

Creating a Virtual Machine:

```
New-AzVM -ResourceGroupName myResourceGroup -Name myVM -Location eastus -Image UbuntuLTS -Credential (Get-Credential)
```

-

Creating a Storage Account:

```
New-AzStorageAccount -ResourceGroupName myResourceGroup -Name mystorageaccount -Location eastus -Sku Standard_LRS
```

-

Scaling Virtual Machines:

```
Set-AzVMSize -ResourceGroupName myResourceGroup -VMName myVM -Size
Standard_DS3_v2
```

-

PowerShell and Scripting

PowerShell scripts are an excellent way to automate Azure management. Here's an example of creating a VM and storage account using a PowerShell script:

```
# Set variables
$resourceGroup = "myResourceGroup"
$location = "eastus"
$vmName = "myVM"
$storageAccount = "mystorageaccount"

# Create resource group
New-AzResourceGroup -Name $resourceGroup -Location $location

# Create storage account
New-AzStorageAccount -ResourceGroupName $resourceGroup -Name
$storageAccount -Location $location -Sku Standard_LRS

# Create virtual machine
New-AzVM -ResourceGroupName $resourceGroup -Name $vmName -Location
$location -Image UbuntuLTS -Credential (Get-Credential)
```

Differences Between Azure CLI and PowerShell

While both Azure CLI and PowerShell can manage Azure resources, there are some key differences:

- **Syntax**: Azure CLI uses a straightforward syntax based on commands like `az vm create`. PowerShell uses cmdlets with a more verbose syntax, like `New-AzVM`.

- **Platform**: Azure CLI is cross-platform and can run on Windows, macOS, and Linux. PowerShell, however, is primarily Windows-based, though it is available on macOS and Linux via PowerShell Core.

- **Scripting**: PowerShell is more powerful for system administration tasks and integrates well with Windows-specific scripts, while Azure CLI is typically simpler for quick commands and automation.

Best Practices for Using Azure CLI and PowerShell

Here are some best practices to ensure your use of Azure CLI and PowerShell is efficient and secure:

1. **Use Resource Group and Tags**: Always organize resources by resource group and use tags for better organization and cost tracking.

2. **Enable Automation**: Automate routine tasks such as resource provisioning and scaling with scripts.

3. **Use Azure Policies**: Enforce consistency and compliance using Azure policies.

4. **Secure Credentials**: Avoid hardcoding sensitive information such as passwords or API keys. Use Azure Key Vault or environment variables.

5. **Leverage Profiles**: Use different profiles for different environments (dev, test, production) to prevent accidental deployment to the wrong environment.

6. **Monitor and Audit**: Always enable monitoring and logging to track the health and usage of your resources.

Conclusion

Both Azure CLI and PowerShell are indispensable tools for managing your Azure resources. Whether you prefer the simplicity of the Azure CLI or the powerful scripting capabilities of PowerShell, mastering these tools will significantly improve your ability to automate, manage, and scale your cloud resources effectively. By understanding the basics of these tools and using them for your daily tasks, you'll be able to work with Azure more efficiently and confidently.

Navigating the Azure Portal

The Azure Portal is the web-based graphical user interface (GUI) that enables users to manage, monitor, and configure all Azure resources. It is a powerful tool that provides visibility and control over your cloud infrastructure and services, and it's often the first place users go when starting with Azure. While automation and scripting tools like Azure CLI and PowerShell are essential, the Portal remains a central hub for exploration, quick setups, troubleshooting, and visual monitoring.

In this section, we will explore how to effectively navigate the Azure Portal, use its key features, manage resources, customize your dashboard, monitor activities, and leverage built-in tools like Cloud Shell and Azure Advisor.

Accessing the Azure Portal

To access the Azure Portal, go to:

https://portal.azure.com

You'll be prompted to log in with your Microsoft or organizational Azure account. Once logged in, you'll land on the **Azure Home Dashboard**.

Key Sections of the Azure Portal

The Azure Portal layout is divided into several sections, each serving a unique purpose:

Global Search Bar

Located at the top of the Portal, the search bar is one of the fastest ways to find resources, services, documentation, and even marketplace products. You can search for:

- Resource names (e.g., `vm-prod-01`)

- Services (e.g., `Virtual Machines`, `App Services`)

- Settings (e.g., `Cost Management`, `Subscriptions`)

- Marketplace items (e.g., `WordPress`, `Ubuntu`, `Datadog`)

Left-Hand Navigation Menu

This menu provides access to commonly used services and areas of the Portal, including:

- **Home** – Your landing page, customizable with shortcuts

- **Dashboard** – Pin and view resources, metrics, and services

- **All Services** – Complete list of Azure services

- **Resource Groups** – Organize and manage collections of resources

- **Subscriptions** – View billing and usage across subscriptions

- **Marketplace** – Deploy applications or templates from Microsoft and partners

You can customize the navigation pane to pin your frequently used services for quick access.

Service Blade and Resource Overview

When you click on a service (e.g., Virtual Machines), a **blade** opens on the right. Blades are dynamic panels that show contextual information and options related to the item selected.

A **Resource Overview** blade contains key information such as:

- Resource name

- Resource group

- Region

- Status (Running, Stopped, etc.)

- Pricing tier

- Tags

- Monitoring metrics

- Quick access to related features (e.g., Restart, Delete, Scale)

Each resource type has a tailored blade with specific controls and configuration options.

Creating Resources from the Portal

Azure makes resource creation intuitive through wizards and forms available in the Portal.

Steps to Create a Virtual Machine:

1. Navigate to the **Virtual Machines** service.

2. Click **+ Create > Azure virtual machine**.

3. In the wizard:

   o Choose your subscription and resource group.

   o Provide a VM name.

   o Select the region and availability options.

   o Choose the image (e.g., Ubuntu LTS, Windows Server).

   o Set up administrator credentials.

   o Configure disk options, networking, and monitoring.

4. Click **Review + Create**.

5. Once validated, click **Create**.

You can monitor deployment progress in the **Notifications** pane (bell icon at the top).

All Azure services follow a similar pattern for resource creation.

Customizing Dashboards

The Dashboard feature in the Azure Portal allows you to create personalized views of your environment.

Creating a Custom Dashboard:

1. From the **Dashboard** tab, click **+ New dashboard**.

2. Give your dashboard a name.

3. Use the **Tile Gallery** to drag and drop elements such as:

    o Resource metrics (e.g., CPU usage for a VM)

    o Charts

    o Lists of resources or services

    o Markdown notes

4. Click **Save** when done.

5. Share your dashboard with a team using **Share > Publish**.

Dashboards are useful for operations teams, developers, and managers who need to monitor environments at a glance.

Monitoring and Insights

Monitoring is one of the most critical tasks in managing cloud infrastructure. Azure provides rich monitoring features within the Portal:

Azure Monitor

- Tracks metrics (CPU, memory, disk I/O), logs, alerts, and diagnostics.

- Accessible from any resource overview blade via the **Monitoring** tab.

Application Insights

- Provides detailed telemetry for web applications.

- Includes page load times, request rates, failure rates, and performance bottlenecks.

Activity Log

- Shows all operations performed on resources within a subscription.

- Useful for auditing and troubleshooting.

- Navigate via **Monitor > Activity Log**.

Setting Alerts

1. Go to **Monitor > Alerts**.

2. Click **+ New Alert Rule**.

3. Define the resource, condition (e.g., CPU > 80%), and action group (e.g., email or webhook).

4. Name and save the alert.

Alerts help detect and respond to issues automatically.

Azure Resource Management

Managing and organizing resources through the Portal is straightforward.

Working with Resource Groups

- View all resources in a group

- Perform bulk actions (e.g., tag, delete)

- Apply **Locks** to prevent accidental deletion:

    ○ Navigate to a resource group

    ○ Go to **Locks > Add**

    ○ Choose **Delete** or **Read-only**

Applying Tags

Tags are metadata elements that help organize and categorize resources.

Example: Apply a tag `Environment=Production`

- Go to a resource > **Tags** > Add tag

- Use consistent naming conventions to enable cost analysis and filtering

Moving Resources

You can move resources between resource groups or subscriptions:

- Navigate to the resource group

- Select **Move > Move to another resource group**

- Choose the destination group and confirm

Note: Not all resource types are movable.

Using Azure Cloud Shell

Azure Cloud Shell is an integrated terminal in the Azure Portal with Azure CLI, PowerShell, Git, and popular tools pre-installed.

To launch Cloud Shell:

1. Click the **Terminal** icon on the top navigation bar.

2. Choose **Bash** or **PowerShell**.

3. If prompted, create a storage account for session persistence.

You can use Cloud Shell to:

- Run scripts

- Manage resources

- Deploy templates

- Interact with GitHub or Azure Repos

Example:

```
az group create --name dev-rg --location westeurope
```

This allows for quick operations without leaving the Portal.

Azure Marketplace and Templates

The **Azure Marketplace** offers hundreds of preconfigured applications and services that can be deployed with a few clicks.

Examples include:

- WordPress

- Jenkins

- Redis

- SAP on Azure

- Third-party security appliances

Navigate to **Marketplace**, search for your desired service, and follow the deployment wizard.

You can also use **Quickstart Templates** for deploying complex solutions via **Resource Manager Templates (ARM)**. These are found under **Templates** in the Portal.

Azure Advisor

Azure Advisor provides personalized recommendations to optimize your resources across four categories:

- **High Availability**

- **Security**

- **Performance**

- **Cost**

Access it via the left-hand menu or search for **Advisor**. Review recommendations and take suggested actions such as:

- Resize underutilized VMs

- Enable backup for critical resources

- Implement just-in-time (JIT) access

- Apply network security best practices

This tool helps you continuously improve your environment's reliability and cost-efficiency.

Keyboard Shortcuts and Productivity Tips

Speed up your Portal navigation using keyboard shortcuts:

- **G + D**: Go to Dashboard

- **G + R**: Go to Resource groups

- **G + C**: Go to All resources

- **/ (Slash)**: Focus on Search bar

Other productivity tips:

- Use **Bookmarks** for frequently used resources

- Create **Tags** for billing and automation

- Save queries in **Log Analytics** for reuse

Conclusion

The Azure Portal is more than just a graphical interface—it's a fully-featured platform for managing, monitoring, and optimizing your cloud infrastructure. Whether you're provisioning a new virtual machine, monitoring application performance, or setting up alerts, the Portal makes it accessible and intuitive.

Mastering the Azure Portal will help you:

- Navigate and locate services quickly

- Perform day-to-day operations efficiently

- Visualize and track resource usage

- Deploy and configure services with minimal setup

- Integrate monitoring, security, and cost optimization

While CLI and automation are vital for advanced workflows, the Portal remains a crucial tool for rapid exploration, configuration, and insight into your Azure environment.

Development Tools and SDKs

Effective cloud development demands the right set of tools. Whether you're deploying web apps, crafting APIs, writing serverless functions, or provisioning infrastructure, Microsoft Azure offers a rich ecosystem of development tools and software development kits (SDKs) to support a wide variety of languages, frameworks, and workflows.

In this section, we'll explore the most commonly used development tools, discuss the official Azure SDKs, and walk through how to configure your local development environment for cloud-native development. We'll also cover best practices, integrations with popular IDEs, version management, and container tooling.

Core Development Tools for Azure

Azure provides native tools to help developers create, deploy, and manage their applications efficiently. Below are the essential development tools every Azure developer should be familiar with.

Visual Studio Code (VS Code)

VS Code is a lightweight, cross-platform code editor developed by Microsoft. It offers:

- IntelliSense for multiple languages

- Integrated terminal and Git

- Azure extensions for seamless cloud integration

- Built-in debugger and task runner

- Remote development via SSH, WSL, or Containers

Install it from https://code.visualstudio.com

Key Azure Extensions:

- **Azure Account** – Login and manage subscriptions

- **Azure App Service** – Deploy and manage web apps

- **Azure Functions** – Create, run, and debug functions

- **Azure Storage** – Explore and upload/download blobs

- **Azure Terraform** – Syntax highlighting, linting, and provisioning tools

Visual Studio (Windows)

Visual Studio 2022+ is ideal for .NET developers building enterprise applications. It provides:

- Full-stack ASP.NET, Blazor, and Xamarin support

- Direct publishing to Azure App Services and Azure Functions

- GUI-based Azure Resource Manager (ARM) template editing

- Azure DevOps and GitHub integration

- Advanced debugging and profiling tools

Example: Publish an ASP.NET project directly to Azure App Service by right-clicking the project → **Publish** → **Azure**.

Azure SDKs

Microsoft provides a wide range of **Azure SDKs** for programming languages including .NET, JavaScript, Python, Java, Go, and more. These SDKs simplify authentication, resource management, storage interaction, and service integration.

Installing SDKs

.NET SDK:

```
dotnet new console -n AzureSampleApp
cd AzureSampleApp
dotnet add package Azure.Storage.Blobs
```

JavaScript/TypeScript SDK (Node.js):

```
npm install @azure/storage-blob
```

Python SDK:

```
pip install azure-storage-blob
```

Java SDK (Maven):

```xml
<dependency>
  <groupId>com.azure</groupId>
  <artifactId>azure-storage-blob</artifactId>
  <version>12.21.0</version>
</dependency>
```

These SDKs follow a consistent naming and design pattern across languages and are versioned to track Azure service updates.

Example: Using Azure Blob Storage SDK

Python:

```python
from azure.storage.blob import BlobServiceClient

connection_string = "<your-connection-string>"
blob_service_client =
BlobServiceClient.from_connection_string(connection_string)
container_client = blob_service_client.get_container_client("my-
container")

with open("example.txt", "rb") as data:
    container_client.upload_blob(name="example.txt", data=data)
```

Node.js:

```javascript
const { BlobServiceClient } = require('@azure/storage-blob');

const blobServiceClient =
BlobServiceClient.fromConnectionString(process.env.AZURE_STORAGE_CON
NECTION_STRING);
const containerClient = blobServiceClient.getContainerClient("my-
container");

async function uploadBlob() {
    const blockBlobClient =
containerClient.getBlockBlobClient("example.txt");
    await blockBlobClient.uploadFile("example.txt");
}
```

```
uploadBlob();
```

These SDKs abstract away REST API complexities and offer first-class async and sync support.

Language and Runtime Support

Azure supports almost every major language. Here's a quick mapping of supported runtimes and where they shine:

Language	Best for	Azure Services
.NET	Enterprise, APIs, Functions	App Service, Functions, AKS, Azure DevOps
JavaScript	Web apps, Functions, APIs	App Service, Functions, Static Web Apps
Python	Data science, automation, APIs	Functions, ML, Data Factory
Java	Enterprise apps, APIs	App Service, Spring Apps, AKS
Go	System programming, microservices	Containers, AKS, CLI tools
PHP	CMS systems, small web apps	App Service, VMs
Ruby	APIs, Web apps	Containers, App Service

Azure provides built-in support for many of these in App Service and Functions. Others may require containerization.

Working with Containers and Docker

For more control over your runtime, **containerization** is often the preferred approach.

Installing Docker

Install Docker Desktop from https://www.docker.com/products/docker-desktop

Verify installation:

```
docker --version
```

Sample Dockerfile for a Node.js App

```
FROM node:18
WORKDIR /app
COPY package*.json ./
RUN npm install
COPY . .
CMD ["node", "index.js"]
```

Build and run locally:

```
docker build -t myapp .
docker run -p 3000:3000 myapp
```

Push to **Azure Container Registry**:

```
az acr login --name myregistry
docker tag myapp myregistry.azurecr.io/myapp:v1
docker push myregistry.azurecr.io/myapp:v1
```

Deploy to **Azure Kubernetes Service (AKS)** or **Azure App Service for Containers**.

Infrastructure as Code (IaC) Tools

Azure supports multiple IaC tools to manage your resources declaratively.

Azure Bicep

Install via CLI:

```
az bicep install
```

Example `main.bicep`:

```
resource rg 'Microsoft.Resources/resourceGroups@2021-04-01' = {
  name: 'my-rg'
  location: 'eastus'
```

```
}
```

Deploy:

```
az deployment sub create --location eastus --template-file
main.bicep
```

Terraform

Install Terraform and initialize a config:

```
provider "azurerm" {
  features = {}
}

resource "azurerm_resource_group" "example" {
  name     = "my-rg"
  location = "East US"
}
```

Initialize and apply:

```
terraform init
terraform apply
```

GitHub and Azure DevOps Integrations

Modern cloud development includes DevOps. Azure supports deep integration with:

- **GitHub Actions** for CI/CD pipelines

- **Azure DevOps Repos, Pipelines, Boards, and Artifacts**

- **Git integration** directly in VS Code and Azure Portal

Example: GitHub Actions workflow for Azure Web App:

```
name: Build and Deploy

on:
  push:
```

```
    branches:
      - main

jobs:
  build-and-deploy:
    runs-on: ubuntu-latest
    steps:
      - uses: actions/checkout@v2
      - name: Set up Node.js
        uses: actions/setup-node@v2
        with:
          node-version: '18'
      - run: npm install && npm run build
      - name: Deploy to Azure
        uses: azure/webapps-deploy@v2
        with:
          app-name: 'myapp'
          publish-profile: ${{ secrets.AZURE_WEBAPP_PUBLISH_PROFILE
}}
          package: '.'
```

Azure CLI and PowerShell Integration

You can use CLI and PowerShell directly from your dev tools:

- Run az commands from VS Code's terminal

- Use Azure PowerShell inside Cloud Shell or locally

- Combine SDKs and CLI for scripting hybrid workflows

Example: Deploy a resource group with CLI inside a script:

```
#!/bin/bash
az login --identity
az group create --name my-dev-group --location westus
```

Best Practices for Tooling Setup

- Use **virtual environments** (Python) or **nvm** (Node.js) to manage runtime versions.

- Store secrets in **Azure Key Vault**, not in environment variables or code.

- Use **pre-commit hooks** to enforce formatting and linting.

- Automate testing and deployment through **CI/CD pipelines**.

- Tag and name resources using consistent conventions.

Summary

The Azure development ecosystem is expansive and flexible. With robust SDKs, powerful IDE extensions, containerization support, and seamless DevOps integrations, developers can work in the languages and environments they prefer—while leveraging Azure's cloud capabilities.

Key takeaways:

- Set up VS Code or Visual Studio with Azure extensions

- Use SDKs appropriate for your language

- Leverage CLI, PowerShell, and IaC tools for repeatable workflows

- Containerize when needed for portability and consistency

- Integrate with GitHub or Azure DevOps for automated deployments

By equipping yourself with the right tools and SDKs, you enable faster, more reliable, and scalable development workflows—built for the cloud from day one.

Chapter 3: Core Azure Services for Developers

Azure App Services

Azure App Services is one of the most essential and versatile offerings for developers building modern web applications and APIs. It is a fully managed Platform as a Service (PaaS) that allows you to host web apps, RESTful APIs, and mobile backends in your preferred programming language without worrying about infrastructure management. This section provides a deep dive into Azure App Services—how it works, its core features, supported stacks, scaling options, deployment methods, security integrations, and best practices.

What Is Azure App Service?

Azure App Service enables developers to quickly build, deploy, and scale enterprise-grade web applications in a fully managed hosting environment. It abstracts away the complexities of managing underlying infrastructure such as virtual machines, load balancers, and network configurations, so developers can focus solely on writing and shipping code.

Key Capabilities:

- Multi-language support (.NET, Java, Node.js, PHP, Python, Ruby)

- Auto-scaling and high availability (including zone redundancy)

- Custom domain and SSL support

- Continuous deployment from GitHub, Azure DevOps, Bitbucket, etc.

- Integration with Azure services (Key Vault, Azure AD, Application Insights)

- Built-in load balancing and traffic routing

App Service Plans

An **App Service Plan** defines the region, features, and capacity of the computing resources for your web app.

Tiers Available:

- **Free (F1)**: Shared compute, basic testing only

- **Shared (D1)**: Shared compute with limited scaling

- **Basic (B1-B3)**: Dedicated compute for low-traffic production workloads

- **Standard (S1-S3)**: Auto-scaling, custom domains, SSL

- **Premium (P1v3–P3v3)**: Enhanced performance, VNet integration, zone redundancy

- **Isolated (I1-I3)**: Private environments using App Service Environment (ASE)

Create a Standard plan using Azure CLI:

```
az appservice plan create \
  --name MyPlan \
  --resource-group MyResourceGroup \
  --sku S1 \
  --is-linux
```

Creating and Deploying a Web App

Step-by-step via Azure CLI:
```
# Create resource group
az group create --name MyResourceGroup --location eastus

# Create App Service plan
az appservice plan create --name MyPlan --resource-group
MyResourceGroup --sku B1 --is-linux

# Create web app
az webapp create --resource-group MyResourceGroup --plan MyPlan --
name mywebapp123 --runtime "NODE|18-lts"
```

This deploys a Node.js web app on Linux. The runtime string format is
`"LANGUAGE|VERSION"`.

Supported Languages and Frameworks

Azure App Service supports a wide range of programming languages:

- **.NET & .NET Core** – Native support for ASP.NET, Razor Pages, MVC

- **Java** – Tomcat, JBoss, WAR deployment

- **Node.js** – Express, NestJS, server-side rendering frameworks

- **Python** – Flask, Django

- **PHP** – Laravel, CodeIgniter

- **Ruby** – Rails, Sinatra (via custom containers)

If you use a language or runtime not natively supported, you can deploy via **custom containers**.

Deployment Options

Azure App Services integrates with several deployment models:

1. GitHub Actions

Azure App Services can trigger deployments automatically on code pushes using GitHub Actions.

```
# .github/workflows/deploy.yml
name: Deploy to Azure Web App
on:
  push:
    branches:
      - main
jobs:
  deploy:
    runs-on: ubuntu-latest
    steps:
    - uses: actions/checkout@v2
    - name: Setup Node.js
      uses: actions/setup-node@v2
      with:
        node-version: '18'
    - run: npm install && npm run build
    - name: Deploy
      uses: azure/webapps-deploy@v2
      with:
```

```
app-name: 'mywebapp123'
publish-profile: ${{ secrets.AZURE_WEBAPP_PUBLISH_PROFILE }}
package: '.'
```

2. Local Git

```
az webapp deployment source config-local-git \
  --name mywebapp123 \
  --resource-group MyResourceGroup
```

Azure returns a Git URL. Push code to it to trigger deployment.

3. Zip Deployment

```
az webapp deployment source config-zip \
  --resource-group MyResourceGroup \
  --name mywebapp123 \
  --src myapp.zip
```

4. FTP/FTPS – Traditional method for legacy deployments.

Scaling and Availability

Azure App Services allows scaling both **vertically** (better plans) and **horizontally** (more instances):

Manual Scaling:

```
az webapp scale --name mywebapp123 --resource-group MyResourceGroup
--number-of-workers 3
```

Auto-Scaling:

Available on Standard and Premium plans via **rules**:

- CPU usage > 70%

- Request count > 1000

- Custom metrics

Use the Azure Portal or ARM templates to define scaling rules.

Custom Domains and SSL

App Services support custom domains and TLS/SSL certificates.

Map Custom Domain:

```
az webapp config hostname add \
  --webapp-name mywebapp123 \
  --resource-group MyResourceGroup \
  --hostname www.mycustomdomain.com
```

Bind SSL Certificate:

1. Upload the certificate in PFX format.

2. Bind it to the domain using the portal or CLI.

Let's Encrypt integration is also available via App Service Extensions.

Authentication and Authorization

Azure App Service has **built-in authentication/authorization** (EasyAuth), which supports:

- Azure Active Directory

- Microsoft Account

- Facebook

- Google

- Twitter

- GitHub

- Custom Identity Providers via OpenID Connect

Enable via:

- Azure Portal > Authentication > Add Identity Provider

- Configure scopes, redirects, and role mapping

Also supports access restrictions by IP or service endpoints.

Environment Variables and App Settings

Define app-specific settings in the Azure Portal or via CLI:

```
az webapp config appsettings set \
  --name mywebapp123 \
  --resource-group MyResourceGroup \
  --settings ENVIRONMENT=production API_KEY=abc123
```

These settings are available in your app's runtime via `process.env` (Node.js), `os.environ` (Python), or `Environment.GetEnvironmentVariable()` (.NET).

Continuous Monitoring with Application Insights

Application Insights integrates with App Services to provide telemetry data:

- Request rates

- Server response times

- Failed requests

- Exception tracking

- Live metrics

Enable it during deployment or post-deployment via:

```
az monitor app-insights component create \
  --app mywebapp123-insights \
  --location eastus \
  --resource-group MyResourceGroup \
  --application-type web
```

Then link it to the web app:

```
az webapp config appsettings set \
  --name mywebapp123 \
```

```
--resource-group MyResourceGroup \
--settings APPINSIGHTS_INSTRUMENTATIONKEY=<instrumentation_key>
```

Diagnostics and Logging

Azure App Service provides:

- **Console logs**

- **HTTP logs**

- **Application logs**

- **Crash dumps**

- **Custom logs**

Enable logging via:

```
az webapp log config \
  --name mywebapp123 \
  --resource-group MyResourceGroup \
  --application-logging true \
  --level information
```

Stream logs:

```
az webapp log tail --name mywebapp123 --resource-group
MyResourceGroup
```

Logs can be directed to storage accounts, blob storage, or exported to Log Analytics.

Staging Slots and Blue-Green Deployments

App Service offers **deployment slots**—live environments for staging, testing, or QA.

- Swap production with staging to do blue-green deployments.

- Route partial traffic for canary releases.

Create a slot:

```
az webapp deployment slot create \
  --name mywebapp123 \
  --resource-group MyResourceGroup \
  --slot staging
```

Swap slots:

```
az webapp deployment slot swap \
  --name mywebapp123 \
  --resource-group MyResourceGroup \
  --slot staging \
  --target-slot production
```

Best Practices for App Service

- Use **staging slots** for safe deployments.

- Enable **Application Insights** from day one.

- Use **Managed Identity** for secure access to resources like Key Vault.

- Configure **Auto-scaling** based on workload.

- Store secrets in **Key Vault**, not in environment variables.

- Apply **network restrictions** for internal-only access if required.

- Use **Custom Health Checks** to ensure your app is responding.

Summary

Azure App Services empowers developers to build and host scalable, secure, and high-performing web applications with minimal infrastructure management. It's the go-to choice for many developers due to its ease of use, extensive language support, built-in DevOps capabilities, and tight integration with the broader Azure ecosystem.

Key takeaways:

- Fully managed hosting with PaaS benefits

- Support for multiple programming languages

- Integrated CI/CD and GitHub Actions support

- Built-in scaling, monitoring, and authentication

- Ideal for both startups and enterprise-grade applications

In the next section, we will explore **Azure Functions**, another powerful tool for building serverless applications that scale automatically based on demand.

Azure Functions (Serverless Computing)

Azure Functions is Microsoft's serverless compute platform, allowing developers to run event-driven code without the need to explicitly provision or manage infrastructure. It's an ideal solution for building lightweight APIs, processing data streams, orchestrating workflows, and responding to system events in real-time. With built-in scaling, pay-per-use pricing, and seamless integrations with other Azure services, Azure Functions offers both simplicity and power.

This section explores the fundamentals of Azure Functions, key use cases, runtime models, programming models, deployment strategies, performance considerations, security integrations, and best practices for developing modern, scalable serverless solutions.

What Is Azure Functions?

Azure Functions is a **Function-as-a-Service (FaaS)** offering that allows developers to execute small pieces of code, called "functions," in response to a wide range of triggers. It is serverless, meaning:

- No need to manage servers or virtual machines

- Automatic scaling based on load

- Execution-based pricing (pay only for the resources you consume)

- Fast deployment and high availability out of the box

Azure Functions supports various languages including:

- JavaScript/TypeScript (Node.js)

- C# (.NET Core and .NET 5/6/7)

- Python

- Java

- PowerShell

- Go (preview)

- Custom handlers (any language over HTTP)

Key Concepts

Trigger

A trigger is what causes the function to execute. Each function must have exactly one trigger. Examples include:

- HTTP request (HTTP Trigger)

- New blob in Azure Storage (Blob Trigger)

- New message in a queue (Queue Trigger)

- Timer schedule (Timer Trigger)

- Event Grid event (Event Grid Trigger)

- Cosmos DB change feed (Cosmos DB Trigger)

Bindings

Bindings are a way to declaratively connect resources to the function. You can have input and output bindings.

- Input binding: reads data from a source (e.g., blob, queue)

- Output binding: writes data to a destination (e.g., database, queue)

Bindings simplify your code by abstracting away connection logic.

Hosting Plans

Azure Functions offers multiple hosting options, each suited to different workloads:

Hosting Plan	Description
Consumption Plan	Auto-scales, pay only for execution time
Premium Plan	Always-ready instances, VNET support, faster performance
Dedicated (App Service)	Runs on an App Service Plan, suitable for heavy apps needing full control
Kubernetes (AKS)	Run Functions on your own Kubernetes cluster using KEDA

For most serverless applications, the **Consumption Plan** is the preferred choice.

Creating Your First Azure Function

Azure Functions can be created in many ways: via the Azure Portal, Azure CLI, Visual Studio, VS Code, or ARM/Bicep templates. Below is a walkthrough using the **Azure CLI** and **VS Code**.

Step 1: Install the Azure Functions Core Tools

```
npm install -g azure-functions-core-tools@4 --unsafe-perm true
```

Step 2: Create a Function App

```
func init my-function-app --worker-runtime node --language
javascript
cd my-function-app
func new --name HttpExample --template "HTTP trigger"
```

Step 3: Run Locally

```
func start
```

You'll see output like:

```
Http Function HttpExample: [GET,POST]
http://localhost:7071/api/HttpExample
```

Step 4: Deploy to Azure

```
az functionapp create \
  --resource-group myResourceGroup \
  --consumption-plan-location eastus \
  --runtime node \
  --functions-version 4 \
  --name myuniquefunctionapp \
  --storage-account mystorageacct

func azure functionapp publish myuniquefunctionapp
```

Triggers and Bindings in Detail

HTTP Trigger Example (Node.js)

```
module.exports = async function (context, req) {
    context.log('HTTP trigger received:', req.body);

    const name = req.body.name || 'world';
    context.res = {
        status: 200,
        body: `Hello, ${name}!`
    };
};
```

Timer Trigger Example (C#)

```
public static void Run([TimerTrigger("0 */5 * * * *")] TimerInfo
myTimer, ILogger log)
{
    log.LogInformation($"Function executed at: {DateTime.Now}");
}
```

This function runs every 5 minutes.

Queue Trigger Example (Python)

```
import logging

def main(msg: func.QueueMessage) -> None:
```

```
    logging.info(f'Queue message received:
{msg.get_body().decode()}')
```

Developing with Azure Functions in VS Code

1. Install the **Azure Functions extension**.

2. Create a new project via Command Palette: `Azure Functions: Create New Project`.

3. Select your language, runtime, and trigger.

4. Use local emulation for development and debugging.

5. Deploy using `Azure Functions: Deploy to Function App`.

Integrating with Other Azure Services

Azure Functions integrates natively with:

- **Azure Event Grid** – for reactive programming models

- **Azure Service Bus** – for enterprise-grade messaging

- **Azure Cosmos DB** – for real-time stream processing

- **Azure Blob Storage** – for file and data processing

- **Azure Key Vault** – for managing secrets securely

- **Azure API Management** – for publishing APIs

These integrations are accomplished using bindings or SDKs and simplify development significantly.

Security and Authentication

Securing Azure Functions is critical, especially HTTP-triggered ones.

Authentication Options:

- **Function Key**: Shared secret passed via headers or query strings

- **Anonymous**: No security (for public APIs or development)

- **Admin Key**: Master key with elevated permissions

- **Azure AD Authentication**: Enable from App Service Authentication settings

- **API Management**: Protect your functions behind an API gateway

Example Secured URL:

```
https://<appname>.azurewebsites.net/api/HttpExample?code=xyz123abc==
```

Store secrets and credentials in **Azure Key Vault** and reference them using **Managed Identity** to avoid hardcoding.

Monitoring and Diagnostics

Azure Functions can emit telemetry data to **Application Insights**, offering:

- Request traces

- Dependency tracking

- Exception logs

- Live metrics

- Custom events

Enable Application Insights:

```
az monitor app-insights component create \
  --app my-function-insights \
  --location eastus \
  --resource-group myResourceGroup
```

Add instrumentation key to your function settings:

```
az functionapp config appsettings set \
  --name myuniquefunctionapp \
  --resource-group myResourceGroup \
```

```
--settings APPINSIGHTS_INSTRUMENTATIONKEY=<your-key>
```

Or let Azure handle it automatically during creation.

Durable Functions

Durable Functions is an extension of Azure Functions that enables **stateful workflows**.

Key patterns:

- **Function chaining**

- **Fan-out/fan-in**

- **Human interaction**

- **Timers and reminders**

Example:

```
[FunctionName("OrchestrationFunction")]
public static async Task Run(
    [OrchestrationTrigger] IDurableOrchestrationContext context)
{
    var output1 = await context.CallActivityAsync<string>("TaskA",
null);
    var output2 = await context.CallActivityAsync<string>("TaskB",
output1);
    return output2;
}
```

Durable Functions are ideal for complex orchestrations with checkpoints and retries.

Performance and Scaling

Azure Functions is designed to **scale automatically** based on:

- Number of incoming events or HTTP requests

- Size of queue or event hub messages

- Timer intervals (concurrent executions)

Considerations:

- Cold starts in Consumption Plan (use Premium to avoid)

- Throttling limits (e.g., memory, file handles)

- Plan quotas and region availability

Use **always-on** for long-running or frequent tasks.

Testing and Debugging

You can test Azure Functions locally with:

- **func start** – runs a local emulator

- **Postman/cURL** – for HTTP trigger testing

- **Azure Storage Explorer** – to simulate blobs and queues

- **Application Insights** – for production observability

VS Code and Visual Studio support breakpoints and step-through debugging.

Deployment Strategies

GitHub Actions

Deploy on every push:

```
uses: Azure/functions-action@v1
with:
  app-name: 'myfunctionapp'
  publish-profile: ${{ secrets.AZURE_FUNCTIONAPP_PUBLISH_PROFILE }}
  package: '.'
```

Azure DevOps Pipelines

Use the **AzureFunctionApp@1** task to build and deploy.

Zip Deploy

```
func azure functionapp publish myuniquefunctionapp --publish-local-
settings -i
```

Best Practices

- Use **async/await** for better concurrency

- Enable **Application Insights** early for telemetry

- Use **durable functions** for orchestrations

- Use **environment variables** for configuration

- Store secrets in **Key Vault**, not in code

- Use **deployment slots** for safe updates

- Set **timeout** appropriately based on plan

- Avoid dependencies with long cold starts

Summary

Azure Functions represents the essence of modern, scalable, event-driven application design. It provides a powerful abstraction for building microservices, APIs, and data processors, all without the overhead of managing servers. With native integrations, diverse trigger support, and seamless CI/CD pipelines, it enables you to focus entirely on code and business logic.

Key takeaways:

- Functions execute in response to events via triggers

- Supports multiple languages and development models

- Native integrations with Azure and third-party services

- Enables stateful workflows with Durable Functions

- Scales automatically with usage

- Perfect for APIs, background jobs, automation, and more

In the next section, we will explore **Azure Storage Solutions**, including Blob Storage, File Storage, and Tables, to understand how to persist and manage data across your applications.

Azure Storage Solutions

Data is at the heart of every application, and Azure offers a comprehensive set of storage services tailored to meet the diverse needs of developers. From unstructured blobs to structured tables, from high-performance file shares to reliable message queues, Azure Storage provides a scalable, durable, and secure platform for storing and managing application data.

This section explores the core Azure Storage services—Blob Storage, Table Storage, Queue Storage, and File Storage. We'll examine their features, use cases, pricing tiers, access methods, and best practices. You'll also learn how to manage storage accounts, secure your data, and interact with storage resources via code, Azure CLI, and SDKs.

Understanding Azure Storage Accounts

A **Storage Account** in Azure is a globally unique namespace that provides access to Azure Storage services. It serves as the parent container for all your data objects and allows you to manage access, monitoring, encryption, and billing.

Types of Storage Accounts

- **General-purpose v2 (GPv2)** – Recommended for most scenarios; supports all storage types.

- **General-purpose v1 (GPv1)** – Legacy version with limited features.

- **Blob storage** – Optimized for storing unstructured data only (legacy).

- **Block blob storage** – Premium performance tier optimized for high-throughput workloads.

- **FileStorage** – Premium file shares only.

Create a Storage Account (CLI)

```
az storage account create \
  --name mystorageacct123 \
  --resource-group myResourceGroup \
```

```
--location eastus \
--sku Standard_LRS \
--kind StorageV2
```

Blob Storage

Blob Storage is designed for storing large amounts of unstructured data such as images, videos, logs, backups, and documents.

Blob Types

- **Block blobs**: Ideal for storing text and binary files.

- **Append blobs**: Optimized for append-only operations (e.g., logging).

- **Page blobs**: Used for VHDs and random read/write operations.

Blob Storage Tiers

- **Hot**: Optimized for frequent access.

- **Cool**: For infrequently accessed data.

- **Archive**: For rarely accessed data with retrieval latency.

Use Cases

- CDN and website assets

- Document management systems

- Backup and recovery.

- Media streaming and data lakes

Uploading a Blob (CLI)

```
az storage blob upload \
  --account-name mystorageacct123 \
  --container-name mycontainer \
  --name photo.jpg \
  --file ./photo.jpg \
  --auth-mode login
```

Sample Code (Python)

```python
from azure.storage.blob import BlobServiceClient

conn_str = "<your_connection_string>"
client = BlobServiceClient.from_connection_string(conn_str)
container = client.get_container_client("images")

with open("cat.jpg", "rb") as data:
    container.upload_blob(name="cat.jpg", data=data)
```

File Storage

Azure Files provides fully managed SMB and NFS file shares in the cloud. It is accessible via standard file protocols, making it a good fit for lift-and-shift migrations, shared file access, and hybrid environments.

Key Features

- Compatible with Windows, Linux, and macOS

- Can be mounted like a network drive

- Supports NTFS ACLs and AD authentication

- Supports snapshots and backups

Use Cases

- File servers and shared folders

- Application logs and config files

- Lift-and-shift legacy apps

- Shared storage for containers or VMs

Mounting an Azure File Share (Linux)

```
sudo mount -t cifs //<storage-account>.file.core.windows.net/<share-
name> /mnt/mountpoint \
  -o vers=3.0,username=<storage-account>,password=<account-
key>,dir_mode=0777,file_mode=0777,serverino
```

Create a File Share (CLI)

```
az storage share create \
  --name myshare \
  --account-name mystorageacct123
```

Table Storage

Azure Table Storage is a NoSQL key-value store for semi-structured data. It is optimized for fast access to large volumes of data and scales automatically.

Data Model

- Data is organized into **tables**

- Each table contains **entities**

- Each entity is a collection of **properties**

- Entities must have **PartitionKey** and **RowKey**

Use Cases

- User profiles

- IoT sensor data

- Auditing and logging

- Product catalogs

Table Storage vs. Cosmos DB Table API

While both support the same APIs, **Azure Table Storage** is more cost-effective but has limited scalability and features. For more advanced scenarios, use **Cosmos DB Table API**.

Inserting Data (Python SDK)

```python
from azure.data.tables import TableServiceClient, TableEntity

service =
TableServiceClient.from_connection_string("<connection_string>")
table_client = service.get_table_client("Products")
```

```
entity = {
    "PartitionKey": "Electronics",
    "RowKey": "SKU12345",
    "Name": "Bluetooth Speaker",
    "Price": 29.99
}
table_client.create_entity(entity=entity)
```

Queue Storage

Queue Storage provides a simple messaging queue for storing and retrieving messages asynchronously between application components. It supports FIFO ordering and is a foundational piece of many distributed architectures.

Features

- Each message can be up to 64 KB

- Queues can store millions of messages

- Guaranteed delivery

- Visibility timeout to hide messages while processing

Use Cases

- Decoupling microservices

- Background job processing

- Event buffering

- Throttling and rate-limiting systems

Creating a Queue and Adding a Message

```
az storage queue create --name taskqueue --account-name
mystorageacct123

az storage message put \
  --queue-name taskqueue \
  --account-name mystorageacct123 \
```

```
--content "Process order #123"
```

Reading a Message (Python)

```python
from azure.storage.queue import QueueClient

client = QueueClient.from_connection_string("<conn_string>",
queue_name="taskqueue")
msg = client.receive_message()
print(f"Message: {msg.content}")
client.delete_message(msg)
```

Securing Storage Accounts

Azure Storage includes several layers of security to protect your data.

Shared Access Signatures (SAS)

Provide granular access to containers, blobs, queues, and files.

```
az storage blob generate-sas \
  --account-name mystorageacct123 \
  --container-name mycontainer \
  --name photo.jpg \
  --permissions r \
  --expiry 2025-12-31T23:59Z \
  --output tsv
```

Use the SAS token in URLs to grant temporary access.

Azure Active Directory Integration

- Use Azure AD to authenticate apps and users

- Define role-based access using RBAC

- Avoid shared keys wherever possible

Private Endpoints

- Connect to storage securely over a private IP

- Isolate traffic within a virtual network

Monitoring and Logging

Monitor storage activity with:

- **Azure Monitor** for metrics (capacity, transactions, latency)

- **Diagnostics settings** to send logs to Log Analytics

- **Alerts** based on storage usage or failure rates

Example alert: Trigger when blob container read operations exceed 10,000 in 15 minutes.

Performance and Scalability Considerations

- Use **Hot tier** for frequent access; use **Cool/Archive** for cost savings

- Parallelize large uploads using **block blobs**

- Use **Content Delivery Network (CDN)** for static content

- For massive datasets, consider **AzCopy** or **Data Box**

Best Practices

- Use **naming conventions** for storage accounts and containers

- Enable **soft delete** for blob recovery

- Use **Managed Identity** to access storage securely

- Avoid using storage account keys directly

- Regularly audit access and rotate keys

- Leverage **lifecycle management policies** to auto-transition data between tiers

Example: Transition blobs to cool tier after 30 days of inactivity:

```json
{
  "rules": [
    {
      "name": "moveToCool",
      "enabled": true,
      "definition": {
        "filters": {
          "blobTypes": [ "blockBlob" ]
        },
        "actions": {
          "baseBlob": {
            "tierToCool": {
              "daysAfterModificationGreaterThan": 30
            }
          }
        }
      }
    }
  ]
}
```

Summary

Azure Storage Solutions provide a foundational building block for cloud-native applications. Whether you need to store media files, stream logs, pass messages, or manage configuration files, Azure has a service tailored for that use case. With built-in security, global scalability, and strong integration with other Azure services, Azure Storage enables developers to build reliable, performant, and maintainable systems.

Key Takeaways:

- Use **Blob Storage** for unstructured data like images and videos

- Use **File Storage** for shared files and lift-and-shift workloads

- Use **Table Storage** for fast, scalable NoSQL storage

- Use **Queue Storage** for decoupled and asynchronous workflows

- Secure your storage using **SAS**, **RBAC**, and **Private Endpoints**

- Monitor and optimize with **Azure Monitor** and **lifecycle policies**

In the next section, we'll cover **Azure SQL and NoSQL Databases,** diving into the managed relational and non-relational database offerings available for developers building data-driven applications.

Azure SQL and NoSQL Databases

Applications of all types—from simple websites to complex, data-intensive platforms—require reliable, secure, and performant databases. Azure offers a robust suite of managed database services, encompassing both traditional relational databases and modern NoSQL options. This allows developers to select the right data model, consistency level, and performance characteristics based on their specific application requirements.

In this section, we'll explore the key database services available on Azure, focusing on **Azure SQL Database** for relational data and **Azure Cosmos DB** for NoSQL workloads. We'll also touch on **Azure Database for PostgreSQL, MySQL,** and **MariaDB,** along with use cases, pricing, performance tuning, scalability, integrations, and security best practices.

Azure SQL Database

Azure SQL Database is a fully managed relational database service built on Microsoft SQL Server. It offers high availability, automated backups, scaling, patching, and security, all without the need to manage the underlying infrastructure.

Deployment Models

1. **Single Database** – Isolated, independently managed database, ideal for microservices or single-tenant apps.

2. **Elastic Pool** – A shared resource model for multiple databases with varying usage patterns.

3. **Managed Instance** – Provides near 100% compatibility with SQL Server, suitable for lift-and-shift scenarios.

Key Features

- Built-in high availability (99.99% SLA)

- Automatic backups with point-in-time restore (up to 35 days)

- Intelligent performance tuning

- Active geo-replication

- Advanced Threat Protection

- VNet integration and Private Link support

Create a SQL Database (CLI)

```
az sql server create \
  --name myserver123 \
  --resource-group myResourceGroup \
  --location eastus \
  --admin-user myadmin \
  --admin-password MyPassword123!

az sql db create \
  --resource-group myResourceGroup \
  --server myserver123 \
  --name mydatabase \
  --service-objective S0
```

Connect Using Connection String

```
string connectionString =
"Server=tcp:myserver123.database.windows.net,1433;Initial
Catalog=mydatabase;User
ID=myadmin;Password=MyPassword123!;Encrypt=True;";
```

Use Cases

- E-commerce platforms

- SaaS applications

- Enterprise applications needing ACID transactions

- Business intelligence and analytics workloads

Performance and Scaling

Azure SQL supports both **provisioned** and **serverless** compute tiers:

- **Provisioned**: Fixed compute size (DTUs or vCores)

- **Serverless**: Automatically scales based on workload, ideal for variable usage

Elastic Pools

Elastic pools allow multiple databases to share resources. They are ideal when:

- Databases have unpredictable usage

- Cost optimization is important

- You manage many databases in a multi-tenant app

Performance Tuning Tools

- **Query Performance Insight** – Analyze query statistics

- **Automatic Indexing** – Create, drop, and tune indexes automatically

- **Intelligent Insights** – Detect and fix performance issues

Security Features

- **Encryption at Rest** with Transparent Data Encryption (TDE)

- **Encryption in Transit** via SSL

- **SQL Firewall** – IP whitelisting and VNet rules

- **Advanced Threat Protection** – Detects SQL injection, brute force, and data exfiltration

- **Azure Defender** – Adds an extra layer of database protection

Configure Firewall Rules

```
az sql server firewall-rule create \
  --resource-group myResourceGroup \
  --server myserver123 \
  --name AllowClientIP \
  --start-ip-address 203.0.113.5 \
  --end-ip-address 203.0.113.5
```

Azure Cosmos DB

Azure Cosmos DB is Microsoft's globally distributed, multi-model NoSQL database service. It's designed for modern applications that demand low latency, high availability, and horizontal scalability.

Supported APIs (Data Models)

- **Core (SQL)** – Document DB model (JSON), similar to MongoDB

- **MongoDB API** – Native MongoDB wire protocol support

- **Cassandra API** – Wide-column model

- **Gremlin API** – Graph-based applications

- **Table API** – Key-value store, compatible with Azure Table Storage

Key Features

- 99.999% availability SLA

- Multi-region writes and replication

- Single-digit millisecond latency

- Five well-defined **consistency levels**

- Automatic and manual scaling

- Built-in TTL, indexing, and partitioning

Provision Cosmos DB (CLI)

```
az cosmosdb create \
  --name mycosmosdb \
  --resource-group myResourceGroup \
  --locations regionName=eastus failoverPriority=0
isZoneRedundant=False \
  --default-consistency-level Session
```

Create a SQL API database and container:

```
az cosmosdb sql database create \
  --account-name mycosmosdb \
```

```
  --resource-group myResourceGroup \
  --name ProductsDB

az cosmosdb sql container create \
  --account-name mycosmosdb \
  --resource-group myResourceGroup \
  --database-name ProductsDB \
  --name ProductsContainer \
  --partition-key-path "/category"
```

Sample Code (Node.js)
```
const { CosmosClient } = require("@azure/cosmos");

const client = new CosmosClient({ endpoint, key });
const container =
client.database("ProductsDB").container("ProductsContainer");

const item = {
    id: "sku-1234",
    name: "Wireless Mouse",
    category: "electronics",
    price: 25.99
};

await container.items.create(item);
```

Consistency Models

Cosmos DB allows you to choose from five consistency levels:

1. **Strong** – Total consistency, reads always return the latest write

2. **Bounded Staleness** – Reads lag behind by a time or operation window

3. **Session** – Consistent reads for a single session (default)

4. **Consistent Prefix** – Reads never see out-of-order writes

5. **Eventual** – Fastest, but no guarantee of order or freshness

Choose the model that best fits your application's latency and correctness requirements.

Global Distribution and Multi-Master Writes

You can replicate Cosmos DB across multiple regions and enable **multi-master writes** for high availability and lower latency.

Enable multi-region writes via:

```
az cosmosdb update \
  --name mycosmosdb \
  --resource-group myResourceGroup \
  --enable-multiple-write-locations true
```

Data is automatically synchronized across regions, and conflicts can be resolved using custom conflict resolution policies.

Azure Database for Open-Source Engines

Azure provides managed services for popular open-source relational databases:

Azure Database for PostgreSQL

- Supports PostgreSQL 11–15

- Flexible server or Hyperscale (Citus)

- Excellent for complex queries, GIS apps, and JSONB support

Azure Database for MySQL

- Supports MySQL 5.7 and 8.0

- Great for LAMP/LEMP stack applications

Azure Database for MariaDB

- Compatible with MySQL clients and tools

These services include:

- Automated patching and backups

- High availability and replication

- SSL enforcement

- Monitoring and performance tuning

Create a PostgreSQL server (CLI):

```
az postgres flexible-server create \
  --resource-group myResourceGroup \
  --name mypgserver \
  --location eastus \
  --admin-user myadmin \
  --admin-password MyPassword123!
```

Choosing the Right Database

Requirement	Recommended Option
Relational schema and ACID support	Azure SQL Database
Global low-latency NoSQL	Azure Cosmos DB
Open-source database compatibility	Azure PostgreSQL/MySQL
Key-value access patterns	Azure Table or Cosmos DB
Horizontal scaling for JSON docs	Cosmos DB SQL API
Complex joins and stored procedures	Azure SQL or PostgreSQL

Security and Compliance

All Azure database services offer enterprise-grade security:

- Network isolation with **Private Link**

- **Encryption at Rest** using service-managed or customer-managed keys

- **Identity-based access control** using Azure Active Directory

- **Threat detection** and **audit logs**

- Compliance certifications: ISO, HIPAA, GDPR, SOC, FedRAMP, and more

Monitoring and Diagnostics

Monitor and optimize databases using:

- **Azure Monitor** for resource metrics

- **Query Performance Insight** for slow queries

- **Workbooks** for visualizations

- **Alerts** for threshold breaches

- **Diagnostics logs** for auditing and debugging

Enable logging:

```
az monitor diagnostic-settings create \
  --resource <resource-id> \
  --name "sql-logs" \
  --logs '[{"category": "SQLInsights", "enabled": true}]' \
  --workspace <log-analytics-workspace-id>
```

Best Practices

- Choose **zone-redundant** or **geo-redundant** databases for critical workloads

- Use **Elastic Pools** to optimize costs in multi-tenant systems

- Use **Stored Procedures** and **Functions** for encapsulating business logic

- Partition Cosmos DB containers with a high-cardinality **partition key**

- Avoid large single-partition workloads; spread writes evenly

- Backup regularly—even if automatic backups are enabled

- Use **retry logic** in client applications to handle transient failures

---

Summary

Azure provides a rich, scalable, and secure ecosystem for both SQL and NoSQL databases. Whether you're building traditional transactional systems, globally distributed NoSQL platforms, or hybrid data architectures, Azure has the tools to support your needs. With built-in intelligence, automation, and integrations, Azure database services empower developers to build modern applications without compromising on performance, availability, or maintainability.

Key Takeaways:

- Use **Azure SQL Database** for managed relational data with minimal overhead

- Choose **Cosmos DB** for global scale, low latency, and NoSQL models

- Consider **PostgreSQL/MySQL** for open-source compatibility

- Optimize performance with **elastic pools**, **partitioning**, and **serverless tiers**

- Secure your data using **RBAC, firewall rules, Private Link**, and **encryption**

- Monitor and scale proactively with **Azure Monitor, Insights**, and **Alerts**

Next, we'll explore **Architecture Patterns** in Chapter 4, starting with microservices and cloud-native design principles for building robust, scalable applications on Azure.

Chapter 4: Building Cloud-Native Applications

Architecture Patterns: Microservices and Beyond

Designing applications for the cloud is not just about moving your code to Azure—it's about embracing a fundamentally new architecture model that thrives in distributed, scalable, and fault-tolerant environments. Cloud-native architecture is built on patterns that enable speed, resilience, elasticity, and continuous delivery.

This section explores modern architecture patterns with a focus on **microservices**, while also covering related and emerging paradigms such as **service mesh**, **event-driven systems**, **serverless components**, and **API-first design**. We'll break down their components, strengths, challenges, and how Azure supports each one through specific services and tooling.

What Is Cloud-Native Architecture?

Cloud-native applications are designed to fully leverage cloud platforms like Azure. Rather than treating the cloud as a remote data center, cloud-native design embraces principles such as:

- **Elastic scalability**

- **Loose coupling**

- **Immutable infrastructure**

- **Infrastructure as code (IaC)**

- **Containerization**

- **Observability and telemetry**

- **Resilience through redundancy and retries**

These principles allow applications to scale horizontally, recover from failure gracefully, and deploy frequently with minimal downtime.

The Microservices Architecture

At the core of most cloud-native designs is the **microservices architecture**—a design where applications are composed of small, independent services that each represent a specific business capability.

Key Characteristics

- **Independently deployable**: Each service can be deployed without affecting others.

- **Decentralized data management**: Each service owns its own database or storage.

- **Technology agnostic**: Services can be written in different languages and use different technologies.

- **Resilience**: Failures in one service don't bring down the entire system.

- **Scalability**: Each service can scale based on its own load characteristics.

Azure Services for Microservices

Component	Azure Service
Container runtime	Azure Kubernetes Service (AKS)
API gateway	Azure API Management, Azure Front Door
Service communication	Azure Service Bus, Azure Event Grid
Database per service	Azure SQL, Cosmos DB, PostgreSQL
Secrets/config	Azure Key Vault, App Configuration
CI/CD	Azure Pipelines, GitHub Actions
Observability	Azure Monitor, Application Insights

Designing Microservices: Domain-Driven Approach

Effective microservices architecture often starts with **Domain-Driven Design (DDD)**. The idea is to break down the application based on **bounded contexts**—areas of business logic that should remain independent.

For example, an e-commerce application could be broken down as:

- **Order Service**

- **Inventory Service**

- **Customer Service**

- **Payment Service**

- **Notification Service**

Each service would have:

- Its own database (polyglot persistence)

- Its own API or message consumer

- Its own lifecycle and deployment cadence

Communication Patterns

Microservices communicate with each other using either:

Synchronous (Request-Response)

- REST APIs (HTTP/S)

- gRPC

Azure Support:

- Azure App Services + API Management

- Azure Functions (HTTP Trigger)

- Azure API Management (Rate limiting, caching, transformation)

Asynchronous (Message/Event Driven)

- Message Queues (e.g., Azure Service Bus)

- Event Streams (e.g., Azure Event Hubs, Event Grid)

Benefits of Asynchronous Patterns:

- Loose coupling

- Improved scalability

- Retry and dead-letter support

Example: Order Service emits an "OrderPlaced" event

- Inventory Service listens and reserves stock

- Notification Service sends a confirmation email

- Analytics Service logs the event

Use **Event Grid** for pub-sub eventing and **Service Bus** for enterprise messaging scenarios with delivery guarantees.

Containerization and Orchestration

Microservices are commonly deployed in containers to ensure consistency, isolation, and easy scaling.

Container Benefits:

- Environment consistency

- Portability across dev/staging/prod

- Faster startup than VMs

- Ideal for immutable deployments

Azure provides:

- **Azure Kubernetes Service (AKS)**: Fully managed Kubernetes

- **Azure Container Apps**: Serverless containers with Dapr integration

- **Azure Container Instances**: Lightweight container runtime for quick jobs

Dockerfile for a Microservice:

```
FROM node:18
WORKDIR /app
```

```
COPY . .
RUN npm install
CMD ["node", "server.js"]
```

Deploy to AKS using Helm or kubectl, or use Container Apps for simplified orchestration.

API Gateways and Service Mesh

As services grow, managing communication, authentication, routing, and observability becomes complex.

API Gateway

Use an API Gateway to:

- Aggregate responses from multiple services

- Transform requests/responses

- Authenticate requests (OAuth, JWT)

- Throttle, cache, and log traffic

Azure Solution: Azure API Management (APIM)

Example:

```
{
  "request": {
    "method": "GET",
    "uri": "/orders/{orderId}"
  },
  "backend": {
    "serviceUrl": "https://orderservice/api/orders/{orderId}"
  }
}
```

Service Mesh

Service Mesh enables:

- Secure service-to-service communication

- Automatic retries and circuit breaking

- Observability and distributed tracing

Azure Solution: **Open Service Mesh (OSM)** on AKS or Dapr with Azure Container Apps

---

Serverless Microservices

Some services can be implemented more efficiently using **serverless functions**:

- Stateless operations

- Lightweight APIs

- Event handlers

- Scheduled tasks

Azure Function Use Cases:

- Payment Webhook Handler

- Send Email on Order Completion

- Cleanup Jobs

- User Registration Trigger

Combine serverless with microservices for cost-efficient scalability.

Event-Driven Architecture

Cloud-native systems often adopt **event-driven design** to decouple producers from consumers.

Benefits:

- Reactive behavior

- Loose coupling

- Real-time processing

- High scalability

Azure Services:

- **Event Grid** – Event delivery with filters and retries

- **Service Bus** – Queues and topics for complex messaging

- **Event Hubs** – High-throughput telemetry ingestion

Use Azure Functions as event consumers for lightweight processing.

Observability and Health Checks

Cloud-native applications must be observable. This includes:

- **Logging**

- **Metrics**

- **Tracing**

- **Health checks**

Azure Tools:

- **Azure Monitor** – Metrics, logs, alerts

- **Application Insights** – Distributed tracing and performance monitoring

- **Log Analytics** – Query logs across services

Use health probes in AKS or App Services to determine pod readiness:

```
livenessProbe:
  httpGet:
    path: /health
    port: 80
  initialDelaySeconds: 30
  periodSeconds: 10
```

CI/CD for Microservices

Each microservice should have its own pipeline. Use templates for repeatability.

Recommended Workflow:

1. Push to GitHub

2. GitHub Action triggers build and test

3. Image pushed to Azure Container Registry

4. Deploy to AKS via Helm or YAML

5. Rollout with canary or blue-green deployment

Example GitHub Actions Workflow:

```
name: Deploy Order Service

on:
  push:
    branches: [main]

jobs:
  build:
    runs-on: ubuntu-latest
    steps:
      - uses: actions/checkout@v2
      - run: docker build -t myregistry/order-service:latest .
      - run: docker push myregistry/order-service:latest
```

Challenges and Tradeoffs

Common Challenges:

- Increased complexity in deployment and communication

- Debugging across multiple services

- Data consistency in distributed systems

- Service discovery and configuration

- Monitoring and tracing in real time

Solutions:

- Use a **Service Mesh** for communication policies

- Implement **centralized logging**

- Use **Saga Pattern** for distributed transactions

- Apply **retry patterns and timeouts** consistently

Best Practices

- Start small: don't break your app into too many microservices prematurely

- Automate everything: builds, tests, deployment, and observability

- Design for failure: implement retries, fallbacks, and circuit breakers

- Isolate faults: keep failures contained within services

- Secure every layer: use mTLS, secrets management, and RBAC

- Keep your services stateless whenever possible

Summary

Microservices and related architecture patterns provide a foundation for building scalable, resilient, and agile cloud-native applications. When combined with Azure's robust service ecosystem—ranging from compute and networking to messaging, storage, and observability—developers can build systems that evolve quickly and scale efficiently.

Key Takeaways:

- Cloud-native architecture is about design, not just deployment

- Microservices provide agility but add operational complexity

- Azure offers rich support for containers, APIs, events, and serverless

- Tools like API Management, Service Bus, and AKS are essential enablers

- Observability, CI/CD, and security must be first-class considerations

In the next section, we'll explore how to **create web APIs with Azure**, focusing on App Services, Azure Functions, and API Management to deliver robust, scalable API layers.

Creating Web APIs with Azure

In the modern software landscape, web APIs are the connective tissue that allows systems, platforms, and applications to communicate. Whether you're building a web frontend, a mobile app, or a suite of microservices, designing and deploying robust APIs is essential. Azure offers a range of services that simplify the creation, deployment, and management of APIs, enabling developers to focus on business logic rather than infrastructure concerns.

This section will explore how to build RESTful APIs on Azure using services such as **Azure App Service**, **Azure Functions**, and **Azure API Management**. We'll cover best practices for API design, authentication and authorization strategies, request validation, versioning, testing, monitoring, and deployment pipelines. By the end, you'll have a comprehensive understanding of how to build enterprise-ready APIs on Azure.

Why Build APIs in Azure?

Azure provides a scalable, secure, and highly available environment for hosting web APIs. Key benefits include:

- Fully managed infrastructure

- Built-in CI/CD integrations

- Native support for serverless and containerized APIs

- Easy integration with authentication providers

- Rich monitoring and analytics with Application Insights

- Support for API gateways and lifecycle management

Whether you're creating REST APIs with .NET Core on App Service or lightweight serverless endpoints with Azure Functions, Azure provides the flexibility to meet your specific needs.

Building APIs with Azure App Service

Azure App Service is a PaaS offering that allows you to host full-fledged web applications and APIs with ease. It supports a wide range of languages including C#, Node.js, Python, Java, and PHP.

Step-by-Step: Deploying a .NET API

1. Create a new ASP.NET Core Web API project:

```
dotnet new webapi -n MyApiApp
cd MyApiApp
```

2. Test it locally:

```
dotnet run
```

3. Create an App Service plan and Web App:

```
az appservice plan create --name MyApiPlan --resource-group MyRG --sku B1 --is-linux
az webapp create --name myapiwebapp --plan MyApiPlan --resource-group MyRG --runtime "DOTNETCORE|6.0"
```

4. Deploy the API:

```
dotnet publish -c Release
az webapp deploy --resource-group MyRG --name myapiwebapp --src-path ./bin/Release/net6.0/publish
```

Your API is now live at:
```
https://myapiwebapp.azurewebsites.net/api/controller
```

Building APIs with Azure Functions

For lightweight APIs or event-driven endpoints, **Azure Functions** is ideal. Functions can be triggered via HTTP requests and scale automatically.

Creating a Function API

1. Initialize a new Function project:

```
func init MyFunctionApi --worker-runtime dotnet
cd MyFunctionApi
func new --name GetProducts --template "HTTP trigger"
```

2. Edit `GetProducts.cs` to return a list:

```
[FunctionName("GetProducts")]
public static IActionResult Run(
    [HttpTrigger(AuthorizationLevel.Function, "get", Route =
"products")] HttpRequest req,
    ILogger log)
{
    var products = new[] {
        new { id = 1, name = "Laptop" },
        new { id = 2, name = "Mouse" }
    };
    return new OkObjectResult(products);
}
```

3. Test locally with:

```
func start
```

4. Deploy using:

```
az functionapp create --resource-group MyRG --name myfunctionapi --
storage-account mystorage --consumption-plan-location westus --
runtime dotnet
func azure functionapp publish myfunctionapi
```

Now accessible at `https://myfunctionapi.azurewebsites.net/api/products`

Designing RESTful APIs

Good API design improves developer experience, maintainability, and scalability.

Key Principles

- **Use nouns in URLs**: /products, not /getProducts

- **Use HTTP methods**: GET, POST, PUT, DELETE

- **Version your APIs**: /v1/products

- **Support filtering, paging, sorting**:
  /products?category=electronics&page=2

- **Return standard HTTP status codes**: 200 OK, 404 Not Found, 500 Internal
  Server Error

Example Routes

Action	Method	Endpoint
Get all products	GET	/api/products
Get one product	GET	/api/products/{id}
Create product	POST	/api/products
Update product	PUT	/api/products/{id}
Delete product	DELETE	/api/products/{id}

API Security and Authentication

Securing your APIs is critical. Azure provides multiple options for securing endpoints:

API Keys

- Use Azure Functions or App Service "Function" auth level

- Embed keys in query strings or headers

OAuth2 and OpenID Connect

- Use Azure Active Directory to secure APIs

- Configure **App Registrations** and **Client Secrets**

Role-Based Access Control (RBAC)

- Use Azure AD groups and role claims

- Implement middleware to check claims per endpoint

Enabling Azure AD Authentication

1. Go to the App Service > Authentication

2. Add Identity Provider > Azure Active Directory

3. Choose app registration or create new

4. Restrict access to authenticated users only

Request Validation and Middleware

Use middleware to validate input and handle common concerns.

ASP.NET Core Example

```
public class ValidateProductMiddleware
{
    private readonly RequestDelegate _next;

    public async Task Invoke(HttpContext context)
    {
        if (context.Request.Method == "POST" &&
context.Request.Path.StartsWithSegments("/api/products"))
        {
            // Validate content-type or JSON body
        }
        await _next(context);
```

```
    }
}
```

Register in `Startup.cs` or `Program.cs`.

API Documentation with OpenAPI

Provide interactive documentation for your API using Swagger/OpenAPI.

In ASP.NET Core

Add NuGet packages:

```
dotnet add package Swashbuckle.AspNetCore
```

Update `Startup.cs`:

```
services.AddSwaggerGen();
app.UseSwagger();
app.UseSwaggerUI(c => {
    c.SwaggerEndpoint("/swagger/v1/swagger.json", "My API V1");
});
```

Navigate to `/swagger` for UI.

Azure Functions Support

Enable OpenAPI through the `Microsoft.Azure.WebJobs.Extensions.OpenApi` package and annotations.

API Monitoring and Logging

Use **Application Insights** to monitor API health and performance.

Enable Insights (CLI)

```
az monitor app-insights component create --app myapiapp --location
eastus --resource-group MyRG --application-type web
```

Track Custom Events

```
var telemetry = new TelemetryClient();
telemetry.TrackEvent("ProductCreated", properties);
```

Log and trace performance:

- Requests

- Failures

- Dependencies (e.g., database calls)

- Custom metrics

API Management with Azure API Management (APIM)

APIM acts as a gateway for your APIs, enabling:

- Centralized routing

- Request/response transformation

- Rate limiting and throttling

- API versioning

- Developer portals

- Policy-based access control

Create APIM (CLI)

```
az apim create --name myapimgateway --resource-group MyRG --
publisher-email admin@example.com --publisher-name "Admin"
```

Import APIs from:

- OpenAPI/Swagger

- Function Apps

- App Services

Define a Policy

Example: Add rate limit

```
<rate-limit-by-key calls="100" renewal-period="60" counter-
key="@(context.Request.IpAddress)" />
```

Deployment and CI/CD

Automate API deployments using GitHub Actions or Azure DevOps.

GitHub Actions Sample

```
name: Build and Deploy API

on:
  push:
    branches: [main]

jobs:
  build-and-deploy:
    runs-on: ubuntu-latest
    steps:
      - uses: actions/checkout@v2
      - name: Setup .NET
        uses: actions/setup-dotnet@v1
        with:
          dotnet-version: '6.0.x'
      - run: dotnet build
      - run: dotnet publish -c Release -o publish
      - uses: azure/webapps-deploy@v2
        with:
          app-name: 'myapiwebapp'
          publish-profile: ${{ secrets.AZURE_WEBAPP_PUBLISH_PROFILE
}}
          package: './publish'
```

Testing APIs

Use tools like:

- **Postman** – For manual testing and scripting

- **REST Client extension** (VS Code) – Save and run .http files

- **Swagger UI** – Try endpoints with real data

- **Unit/integration tests** – Use frameworks like xUnit, Jest, or Mocha

Example xUnit test:

```
[Fact]
public async Task GetProducts_ReturnsOk()
{
    var response = await _client.GetAsync("/api/products");
    Assert.Equal(HttpStatusCode.OK, response.StatusCode);
}
```

Best Practices

- Use **API versioning** from day one

- Return standardized error responses (e.g., ProblemDetails)

- Implement **rate limiting** to prevent abuse

- Monitor all endpoints with Application Insights

- Secure sensitive APIs with **Azure AD**

- Document APIs using **OpenAPI/Swagger**

- Automate builds and deployments using **CI/CD pipelines**

- Design APIs with idempotency and statelessness

Summary

Azure offers powerful capabilities for building modern APIs, whether you prefer traditional web frameworks or serverless functions. With tools like App Service, Azure Functions, and API Management, you can create APIs that are scalable, secure, observable, and developer-friendly. By following industry best practices and leveraging Azure's rich ecosystem, you can deliver high-quality APIs that serve as reliable interfaces for your applications and services.

Key Takeaways:

- Use **App Service** for full-featured APIs

- Use **Azure Functions** for lightweight, event-driven APIs

- Secure APIs with **Azure AD**, API keys, or OAuth2

- Manage APIs at scale using **API Management**

- Monitor APIs with **Application Insights**

- Document and test APIs using **OpenAPI/Swagger**

- Automate deployments via **GitHub Actions** or **Azure DevOps**

Next, we'll explore how to **deploy cloud-native applications via CI/CD pipelines**, ensuring rapid, safe, and repeatable delivery in a cloud-first development workflow.

Deploying Applications via CI/CD Pipelines

Continuous Integration and Continuous Deployment (CI/CD) are essential practices in modern software development that enable rapid, reliable, and repeatable software delivery. In a cloud-native world, CI/CD pipelines ensure that application updates are automatically built, tested, and deployed with minimal human intervention, enabling teams to innovate faster and respond to change more effectively.

Azure provides a wide range of services and integrations to implement CI/CD pipelines, including **GitHub Actions**, **Azure DevOps Pipelines**, and **third-party tools** like Jenkins, CircleCI, and GitLab CI. In this section, we will explore how to build robust CI/CD pipelines in Azure, focusing on deploying web apps, APIs, containers, serverless functions, and infrastructure as code (IaC) using tools like Bicep and Terraform.

CI/CD Overview

- **Continuous Integration (CI)** is the process of automatically building and testing code every time a change is made to a shared repository.

- **Continuous Deployment/Delivery (CD)** ensures that these changes are automatically or semi-automatically deployed to testing, staging, or production environments.

CI/CD goals:

- Reduce manual deployment errors

- Improve deployment speed

- Maintain high-quality software

- Enable faster time-to-market

Azure DevOps Pipelines

Azure DevOps provides powerful pipelines for automating builds and releases. You can configure pipelines as YAML files (code-first) or use the visual designer (GUI).

Components of Azure Pipelines

- **Pipeline**: The definition of your build or release process

- **Stage**: Logical grouping (e.g., Build, Test, Deploy)

- **Job**: Unit of execution within a stage

- **Step**: Task or script

- **Agent**: The compute resource that runs the pipeline

- **Environment**: Target for deployment (e.g., Azure Web App)

Sample Pipeline for .NET Web App

```
trigger:
  branches:
    include:
      - main

pool:
  vmImage: 'windows-latest'

variables:
  buildConfiguration: 'Release'

steps:
```

```
- task: UseDotNet@2
  inputs:
    packageType: 'sdk'
    version: '6.x'
    installationPath: $(Agent.ToolsDirectory)/dotnet

- task: DotNetCoreCLI@2
  inputs:
    command: 'build'
    projects: '**/*.csproj'
    arguments: '--configuration $(buildConfiguration)'

- task: DotNetCoreCLI@2
  inputs:
    command: 'publish'
    publishWebProjects: true
    arguments: '--configuration $(buildConfiguration) --output
$(Build.ArtifactStagingDirectory)'
    zipAfterPublish: true

- task: PublishBuildArtifacts@1
  inputs:
    pathtoPublish: '$(Build.ArtifactStagingDirectory)'
    artifactName: 'drop'
```

GitHub Actions

GitHub Actions is a powerful CI/CD platform integrated directly into GitHub. It supports all major languages and platforms and integrates well with Azure.

Sample GitHub Actions Workflow

```
name: Build and Deploy Web App

on:
  push:
    branches: [ main ]

jobs:
  build-and-deploy:
    runs-on: ubuntu-latest
    steps:
```

```
    - name: Checkout code
      uses: actions/checkout@v3

    - name: Setup .NET
      uses: actions/setup-dotnet@v3
      with:
        dotnet-version: '6.0.x'

    - name: Build project
      run: dotnet build --configuration Release

    - name: Publish project
      run: dotnet publish -c Release -o output

    - name: Deploy to Azure Web App
      uses: azure/webapps-deploy@v2
      with:
        app-name: 'mywebapp123'
        publish-profile: ${{ secrets.AZURE_WEBAPP_PUBLISH_PROFILE
}}
        package: './output'
```

You can securely store deployment credentials using **GitHub Secrets**.

Deploying Azure Functions with CI/CD

Azure Functions support deployment via Zip Deploy, FTP, GitHub Actions, Azure Pipelines, and more.

Azure DevOps Pipeline for Function App

```
trigger:
  branches:
    include:
      - main

pool:
  vmImage: 'ubuntu-latest'

steps:
- task: AzureFunctionApp@1
```

```
inputs:
  azureSubscription: 'MyAzureConnection'
  appType: 'functionApp'
  appName: 'myfunctionapi'
  package: '$(System.DefaultWorkingDirectory)/**/*.zip'
```

You can generate the zip file using the `func` CLI:

```
func azure functionapp publish myfunctionapi --build-native-deps --
publish-local-settings -i
```

Container-Based Deployments

Containers provide portability and are ideal for microservices and Kubernetes-based apps.

Common Workflow:

1. Build Docker image

2. Push to Azure Container Registry (ACR)

3. Deploy to Azure Kubernetes Service (AKS) or Azure Container Apps

GitHub Actions Example:

```
jobs:
  build-and-deploy:
    runs-on: ubuntu-latest
    steps:
      - uses: actions/checkout@v3
      - name: Login to ACR
        uses: azure/docker-login@v1
        with:
          login-server: myregistry.azurecr.io
          username: ${{ secrets.ACR_USERNAME }}
          password: ${{ secrets.ACR_PASSWORD }}

      - name: Build and push image
        run: |
          docker build -t myregistry.azurecr.io/myapp:latest .
          docker push myregistry.azurecr.io/myapp:latest
```

```
    - name: Deploy to AKS
      uses: azure/k8s-deploy@v1
      with:
        manifests: |
          ./manifests/deployment.yaml
```

Infrastructure as Code (IaC) in Pipelines

Managing cloud infrastructure using code ensures consistency and repeatability.

Bicep Template Deployment

Create a `main.bicep` file to provision resources:

```
resource storage 'Microsoft.Storage/storageAccounts@2022-09-01' = {
  name: 'mystorageacct'
  location: 'eastus'
  sku: {
    name: 'Standard_LRS'
  }
  kind: 'StorageV2'
}
```

Deploy with Azure CLI:

```
az deployment group create --resource-group MyRG --template-file
main.bicep
```

Integrate into pipeline:

```
- task: AzureCLI@2
  inputs:
    azureSubscription: 'MyAzureConnection'
    scriptType: 'bash'
    scriptLocation: 'inlineScript'
    inlineScript: |
      az deployment group create --resource-group MyRG --template-
file main.bicep
```

Testing and Quality Gates

Integrate tests into your pipelines:

- **Unit Tests** – Run during build phase

- **Integration Tests** – Run post-deploy to staging

- **Static Code Analysis** – Use tools like SonarQube or ESLint

- **Security Scans** – Use tools like OWASP ZAP or Snyk

.NET Test Example:

```
- task: DotNetCoreCLI@2
  inputs:
    command: 'test'
    projects: '**/*Tests.csproj'
    arguments: '--configuration Release'
```

JavaScript Test Example:

```
- run: npm install
- run: npm test
```

Deployment Strategies

You can use different deployment techniques to minimize risk:

- **Blue-Green Deployment**: Deploy new version to a parallel environment and swap after verification.

- **Canary Releases**: Gradually expose new version to a subset of users.

- **Rolling Updates**: Replace old instances with new ones incrementally.

- **Feature Flags**: Control access to new features without redeploying.

Azure App Service and Azure Front Door support **slot-based deployments**, which allow testing in staging environments before going live.

Notifications and Alerts

Notify teams of pipeline status via:

- **Email notifications**

- **Microsoft Teams/Slack integrations**

- **Azure Monitor alerts**

Teams Integration Example (GitHub Actions):

```
- name: Send Notification to Teams
  uses: skitionek/notify-microsoft-teams@v1
  with:
    webhook_url: ${{ secrets.TEAMS_WEBHOOK }}
    message: '🚀 Deployment completed!'
```

Cost Management in CI/CD

To manage pipeline costs:

- Use **self-hosted agents** for high-volume builds

- Schedule **nightly builds** instead of building on every commit

- Reuse artifacts between stages

- Minimize egress by colocating resources

Best Practices

- Keep pipeline code version-controlled

- Use environment-specific variables/secrets

- Automate rollback on failure

- Run linting and tests before deploying

- Protect main and release branches

- Use templates and reusable workflows for consistency

Summary

CI/CD pipelines are foundational to modern application development. With Azure's extensive ecosystem, you can create powerful, flexible, and secure pipelines that support everything from traditional web apps to containerized microservices and serverless functions. By automating your software delivery lifecycle, you gain speed, confidence, and the ability to innovate continuously.

Key Takeaways:

- Use **Azure DevOps** or **GitHub Actions** for automated CI/CD workflows

- Deploy to Azure App Service, Functions, AKS, or Container Apps with ease

- Integrate **testing**, **linting**, **security**, and **infrastructure as code**

- Adopt advanced strategies like **canary releases** and **blue-green deployments**

- Use **monitoring and alerts** to maintain visibility and control

- Continuously improve pipeline performance and cost-efficiency

In the next section, we'll dive into integrating your CI/CD pipelines with **Azure DevOps**, unlocking deeper project management, artifact storage, and test automation capabilities within Microsoft's comprehensive DevOps toolchain.

Integrating with Azure DevOps

Azure DevOps is Microsoft's comprehensive suite of development tools that enables teams to plan, develop, test, deliver, and maintain applications more effectively. It is a robust, cloud-based platform designed to support the entire software development lifecycle, from code repositories to CI/CD pipelines, testing, artifact storage, and agile planning.

In this section, we will explore how to integrate your development workflow with Azure DevOps. We'll walk through setting up and managing projects, using Azure Repos for source control, building pipelines with Azure Pipelines, deploying applications, managing artifacts, tracking work with Boards, testing with Azure Test Plans, and securing environments. By mastering Azure DevOps integration, you can establish a highly productive and collaborative development environment with streamlined delivery pipelines.

Azure DevOps Overview

Azure DevOps includes the following core services:

- **Azure Boards** – Agile planning tools for work tracking

- **Azure Repos** – Git repositories for version control

- **Azure Pipelines** – CI/CD automation

- **Azure Test Plans** – Manual and exploratory testing tools

- **Azure Artifacts** – Package management for NuGet, npm, Maven, and more

These services can be used together or independently and integrate with other tools like GitHub, Jenkins, Terraform, and more.

Setting Up a Project in Azure DevOps

To begin using Azure DevOps:

1. Navigate to https://dev.azure.com.

2. Sign in with your Microsoft or Azure AD account.

3. Create a new organization or join an existing one.

4. Click **New Project**, give it a name, and choose visibility (private/public).

5. Configure repositories, pipelines, boards, and permissions as needed.

Each project provides a self-contained environment for tracking work, managing code, and deploying applications.

Using Azure Repos for Source Control

Azure Repos offers private Git repositories with support for pull requests, branch policies, and webhooks.

Creating a New Repo

1. Go to **Repos > Files**

2. Click **Initialize with README**, or push an existing repo from your local system:

```
git remote add origin
https://dev.azure.com/yourorg/project/_git/repo
git push -u origin --all
```

Branch Policies

- Enforce pull requests before merging

- Require build pipeline to succeed

- Automatically assign reviewers

- Enforce code coverage and work item linking

Pull Request Example

Use the Azure DevOps UI or CLI to create pull requests and assign reviewers. This encourages code review and fosters collaboration.

Azure Pipelines: CI/CD Automation

Azure Pipelines enables automated builds, tests, and deployments using both **YAML-based pipelines** and **classic pipelines**.

YAML Pipeline Example

```yaml
trigger:
  branches:
    include:
      - main

pool:
  vmImage: ubuntu-latest

steps:
- task: UseDotNet@2
  inputs:
    packageType: sdk
    version: '6.0.x'

- task: DotNetCoreCLI@2
  inputs:
    command: restore
```

```
    projects: '**/*.csproj'

- task: DotNetCoreCLI@2
  inputs:
    command: build
    projects: '**/*.csproj'

- task: DotNetCoreCLI@2
  inputs:
    command: test
    projects: '**/*Tests.csproj'
```

Pipeline Features

- Run on Microsoft-hosted or self-hosted agents

- Parallel jobs and environments

- Secrets and secure variables

- Environment approvals and checks

- Reusable pipeline templates

Deploying Applications from Azure Pipelines

Azure Pipelines supports deploying to various targets:

- **Azure Web Apps**

- **Azure Kubernetes Service (AKS)**

- **Virtual Machines**

- **Azure Functions**

- **Container Registries**

- **Third-party cloud providers**

Deploy to Azure Web App Example

```
- task: AzureWebApp@1
```

```
inputs:
  azureSubscription: 'My Azure Connection'
  appName: 'myappname'
  package: '$(System.ArtifactsDirectory)/drop/*.zip'
```

Azure Boards: Agile Work Management

Azure Boards provides tools for tracking:

- **User stories**

- **Bugs**

- **Tasks**

- **Epics**

- **Sprints and iterations**

Features

- Customizable Kanban and Scrum boards

- Built-in backlogs and sprint planning tools

- Dashboards and widgets

- Queries for filtering and reporting

Example: Creating a New Work Item

1. Go to **Boards > Work Items**

2. Click **New Work Item > User Story**

3. Set Title, Area, Iteration, and assign to a team member

Work items can be linked to commits, pull requests, builds, and deployments for end-to-end traceability.

Azure Test Plans

Azure Test Plans offer manual testing capabilities and tracking.

Features

- Test case management

- Exploratory testing

- Capture screenshots and video

- Feedback and bug logging

- Integration with pipelines and boards

You can create test suites for different features or user journeys, then link them to release pipelines for validation.

Azure Artifacts

Azure Artifacts provides private feeds for storing packages like NuGet, npm, Maven, and Python.

Use Cases

- Hosting internal libraries and SDKs

- Sharing reusable modules across teams

- Versioning and dependency tracking

Example: Connect to NuGet Feed

```
nuget sources Add -Name "MyFeed" -Source
"https://pkgs.dev.azure.com/yourorg/_packaging/yourfeed/nuget/v3/ind
ex.json"
```

Include packages in your build and publish using tasks like NuGetCommand@2.

Integrating External Repositories

Azure Pipelines can integrate with:

- GitHub

- Bitbucket

- GitLab

- GitHub Enterprise

Use the **Service connections** panel to authorize access and trigger pipelines on external commits.

Secrets Management and Security

Store credentials, tokens, and secrets securely in Azure DevOps:

- Use **Pipeline secrets/variables**

- Link to **Azure Key Vault** for secure runtime access

- Set **environment approvals** to prevent unauthorized deployments

Example: Accessing a Secret in a Pipeline

```
variables:
  - group: MySecretGroup

steps:
  - script: echo $(my-secret-key)
```

Monitoring and Reporting

Azure DevOps provides extensive reporting and logging:

- **Build and release history**

- **Test coverage**

- **Pipeline duration metrics**

- **Work item burndown charts**

- **Dashboards with custom widgets**

Create dashboards to visualize sprint progress, deployment frequency, or incident response timelines.

Notifications and Alerts

Stay informed with:

- Email notifications

- Microsoft Teams integration

- Webhooks for third-party services

- Slack and Discord integrations

Configure notification rules for events like:

- Failed builds

- Pull requests created/updated

- Work item changes

Best Practices

- Use **multi-stage YAML pipelines** for consistency

- Apply **branch policies** and **required reviewers**

- Organize code, boards, tests, and pipelines by **microservice or domain**

- Automate **infrastructure** with Bicep or Terraform in pipelines

- Secure pipelines with **approval gates** and **Key Vault integration**

- Use **dashboards** to track team health and delivery velocity

- Define **work item templates** for recurring tasks

Summary

Integrating with Azure DevOps unlocks a powerful and unified development experience. From code hosting and automated testing to secure deployments and agile project tracking, Azure DevOps brings all the tools you need into one collaborative platform. Whether you're working in a small startup or an enterprise-scale team, Azure DevOps helps you accelerate software delivery while maintaining high quality and control.

Key Takeaways:

- Use **Azure Repos** or integrate GitHub for version control

- Automate builds and deployments with **Azure Pipelines**

- Track progress and plan sprints using **Azure Boards**

- Manage manual and exploratory testing with **Azure Test Plans**

- Host and distribute packages via **Azure Artifacts**

- Implement robust DevSecOps practices with **Key Vault**, **RBAC**, and **gated approvals**

In the next chapter, we'll shift focus to **secure and scalable development**—ensuring your Azure-hosted applications are protected, performant, and resilient in real-world production environments.

Chapter 5: Secure and Scalable Development

Authentication and Authorization in Azure

Security is a foundational pillar of any modern application architecture. As applications become more distributed and handle increasingly sensitive data, the importance of robust authentication and authorization mechanisms cannot be overstated. Azure provides a wide array of services, protocols, and best practices to implement identity management and secure access control across your cloud-based applications.

This section explores authentication and authorization concepts, how they are implemented in Azure, and how they can be integrated into different application architectures. We will cover Azure Active Directory (Azure AD), role-based access control (RBAC), managed identities, OAuth 2.0, OpenID Connect, and identity management strategies for web, mobile, serverless, and microservice-based applications.

Understanding Authentication and Authorization

Before diving into Azure-specific implementations, it's important to distinguish between:

- **Authentication**: Verifying a user or service's identity. "Who are you?"

- **Authorization**: Determining what actions a user or service can perform. "What are you allowed to do?"

These mechanisms often work together—once a user is authenticated, they are authorized to perform actions based on their permissions.

Azure Active Directory (Azure AD)

Azure AD is Microsoft's cloud-based identity and access management service. It enables secure access to Azure resources, SaaS apps, and custom applications.

Key Features

- Identity federation with external providers (Google, Facebook, etc.)

- Support for SAML, OAuth 2.0, OpenID Connect, WS-Federation

- Single sign-on (SSO)

- Multi-factor authentication (MFA)

- Conditional Access policies

- Integration with Microsoft Entra and hybrid identities

Use Cases

- Secure user sign-in for applications

- Application-to-application authentication

- Access management for APIs and microservices

- Device and location-based access controls

Registering an Application in Azure AD

To authenticate users or services, register your application in Azure AD.

1. Navigate to **Azure Portal > Azure Active Directory > App registrations**

2. Click **New registration**

3. Provide:

   o Name: MyApp

   o Redirect URI: https://myapp.com/auth/callback

4. Click **Register**

5. Copy the **Application (client) ID** and **Directory (tenant) ID**

Create a **client secret** (for confidential clients):

- Go to **Certificates & secrets**

- Click **New client secret**

- Set expiry duration and copy the secret value

Authentication Flow: OAuth 2.0 and OpenID Connect

Azure AD supports **OAuth 2.0** for authorization and **OpenID Connect (OIDC)** for identity verification.

Authorization Code Flow (Web Applications)

1. Redirect user to Azure AD login

2. User authenticates

3. Azure AD sends an authorization code to the redirect URI

4. App exchanges the code for an access token and ID token

5. Access token is used for API requests

Token Types

- **Access Token**: Grants access to APIs

- **ID Token**: Contains user identity claims

- **Refresh Token**: Retrieves new tokens without user interaction

---

Using MSAL for Authentication

Microsoft Authentication Library (MSAL) enables apps to authenticate with Azure AD.

Install MSAL (JavaScript)

```
npm install @azure/msal-browser
```

Example Login Flow (SPA)

```
import { PublicClientApplication } from "@azure/msal-browser";

const msalConfig = {
  auth: {
    clientId: "your-client-id",
```

```
    authority: "https://login.microsoftonline.com/your-tenant-id",
    redirectUri: "https://yourapp.com",
  }
};

const msalInstance = new PublicClientApplication(msalConfig);

msalInstance.loginPopup({
  scopes: ["User.Read"]
}).then(response => {
  console.log("Access token:", response.accessToken);
});
```

.NET (Confidential Client)

```
var app = ConfidentialClientApplicationBuilder
  .Create(clientId)
  .WithClientSecret(clientSecret)
  .WithAuthority(new Uri(authority))
  .Build();

var result = await app.AcquireTokenForClient(scopes).ExecuteAsync();
```

Azure App Service Authentication (EasyAuth)

Azure App Service provides built-in authentication without writing code.

Enable EasyAuth

1. Go to **App Service > Authentication**

2. Click **Add identity provider**

3. Select **Microsoft**

4. Configure scopes, app registration, and callback URLs

5. Restrict access to authenticated users

EasyAuth adds authentication headers like X-MS-CLIENT-PRINCIPAL-ID to incoming requests.

Benefits

- No middleware setup needed

- Integrates with social providers (Google, Facebook, Twitter)

- Works with Azure Functions and App Services

- Supports role-based claims

Role-Based Access Control (RBAC)

RBAC allows you to control access to Azure resources at a granular level.

Key Concepts

- **Security Principal**: A user, group, service principal, or managed identity

- **Role Definition**: A collection of permissions

- **Scope**: Subscription, Resource Group, or Resource

Built-in Roles

- **Owner** – Full access

- **Contributor** – Can manage resources but not assign roles

- **Reader** – View-only access

- **Storage Blob Data Contributor**, etc.

Assigning a Role (CLI)

```
az role assignment create \
  --assignee <principalId> \
  --role "Contributor" \
  --scope /subscriptions/{subscription-id}/resourceGroups/{resource-
group}
```

RBAC is ideal for controlling infrastructure-level access, not app-level permissions.

Managed Identities

Managed identities enable Azure services to authenticate to other services without credentials.

Types

- **System-assigned**: Bound to a single resource

- **User-assigned**: Shared across resources

Use Case: App Service → Azure Key Vault

1. Enable Managed Identity on App Service

2. Add access policy in Key Vault for that identity

3. Use SDK or REST API with `DefaultAzureCredential`

```
var client = new SecretClient(new
Uri("https://myvault.vault.azure.net/"), new
DefaultAzureCredential());
KeyVaultSecret secret = client.GetSecret("MySecret");
```

No need to store secrets in code or config files.

Authentication for APIs and Microservices

Secure APIs with Azure AD and validate tokens using middleware.

ASP.NET Middleware

```
services.AddAuthentication(JwtBearerDefaults.AuthenticationScheme)
  .AddJwtBearer(options =>
  {
    options.Authority = "https://login.microsoftonline.com/{tenant-id}/v2.0";
    options.Audience = "api://your-api-client-id";
  });
```

API Scopes

In Azure AD:

- Define **exposed scopes** (e.g., `api://your-api-client-id/read`)

- Clients must request these scopes during token acquisition

Authorization Strategies

Claims-Based Authorization

Use claims from the ID token or access token to enforce policies.

```
[Authorize(Policy = "AdminOnly")]
public IActionResult GetAdminData() { ... }
```

Configure policy:

```
services.AddAuthorization(options =>
{
  options.AddPolicy("AdminOnly", policy =>
    policy.RequireClaim("roles", "Admin"));
});
```

Custom Roles in Azure AD

1. Create roles in App Registration > Manifest

2. Assign users to roles in Enterprise Applications

3. Use `roles` claim in access token to enforce access rules

Multi-Tenant Applications

Multi-tenant apps allow users from any Azure AD directory to sign in.

- Set App Registration `signInAudience` to `AzureADMultipleOrgs`

- Use dynamic tenant validation in code

- Restrict access using tenant allow lists

This is common for SaaS applications.

Identity for Frontend and Mobile Apps

SPA (Single Page Applications)

Use **PKCE** (Proof Key for Code Exchange) with MSAL.js

- No client secret needed

- Secure against authorization code interception

Mobile Apps

Use **MSAL for Android/iOS** or **Microsoft.Identity.Client** for Xamarin/MAUI

- Handles token caching and refresh

- Secure against token theft

Testing and Debugging

- Use **jwt.ms** to decode and inspect tokens

- Use **Postman** with OAuth 2.0 flow

- Monitor sign-in events in Azure AD logs

- Use **Fiddler** or **Browser Dev Tools** to inspect redirect and headers

---

Best Practices

- Prefer Azure AD over homegrown authentication

- Use **RBAC and Managed Identities** for Azure services

- Avoid storing secrets in code; use **Key Vault**

- Use **PKCE** for SPAs and mobile apps

- Rotate client secrets and certificates regularly

- Use **Conditional Access** and **MFA** for sensitive applications

- Apply **least privilege** principle across all roles and access controls

- Monitor sign-ins and audit logs for anomalies

Summary

Authentication and authorization are fundamental to building secure applications in Azure. By leveraging Azure AD, OAuth 2.0, managed identities, and RBAC, you can design secure and scalable identity architectures that work across web, mobile, API, and microservice platforms. With Azure's built-in tools and best practices, securing your application has never been more achievable.

Key Takeaways:

- Use **Azure AD** for unified identity management

- Secure APIs with **OAuth 2.0** and **OpenID Connect**

- Implement **RBAC** and **role-based claims** for granular control

- Enable **EasyAuth** for fast authentication on App Services

- Use **Managed Identities** to access Azure services without secrets

- Follow identity best practices for scalability and security

Next, we'll explore how to securely manage application secrets using **Azure Key Vault**, helping you further reduce the risks of data leakage and unauthorized access.

Azure Key Vault and Secrets Management

Managing secrets, keys, certificates, and other sensitive information securely is one of the most critical responsibilities for modern application developers and cloud architects. Improper handling of secrets can lead to data breaches, unauthorized access, and security vulnerabilities that are difficult to detect and mitigate after deployment.

Azure Key Vault provides a centralized, secure, and scalable solution for storing and accessing sensitive configuration data. It integrates seamlessly with other Azure services, supports advanced access policies, and offers fine-grained control over secret lifecycle management.

This section explores the full scope of Azure Key Vault—its core components, use cases, integration patterns, security practices, and implementation strategies for different types of applications including web apps, microservices, containers, and serverless workloads.

What is Azure Key Vault?

Azure Key Vault is a cloud-based service that safeguards cryptographic keys, secrets (like passwords and API keys), and digital certificates. It enables secure storage and access control for sensitive information and helps you comply with standards such as ISO/IEC 27001, FedRAMP, and GDPR.

Core Components

- **Secrets** – Strings like connection strings, passwords, tokens, or any sensitive configuration.

- **Keys** – Cryptographic keys for encryption/decryption and signing.

- **Certificates** – X.509 certificates for TLS, client auth, or other uses.

- **Managed HSM (Hardware Security Module)** – FIPS 140-2 Level 3 compliant HSM for advanced scenarios.

Use Cases

- Storing database connection strings and credentials

- Securing API keys and OAuth tokens

- Managing TLS/SSL certificates and renewals

- Protecting application settings for cloud-hosted apps

- Encrypting sensitive data using customer-managed keys (CMK)

- Signing JSON Web Tokens (JWTs) or documents

Creating a Key Vault

You can create a Key Vault through the Azure Portal, Azure CLI, or ARM/Bicep templates.

Azure CLI Example

```
az keyvault create \
  --name mykeyvault123 \
  --resource-group MyResourceGroup \
  --location eastus \
  --sku standard
```

Storing and Retrieving Secrets

Adding a Secret

```
az keyvault secret set \
  --vault-name mykeyvault123 \
  --name "DbConnectionString" \
  --value "Server=mydb;User Id=admin;Password=secret123"
```

Retrieving a Secret

```
az keyvault secret show \
  --vault-name mykeyvault123 \
  --name "DbConnectionString" \
  --query value
```

Secrets are versioned automatically. Older versions can be retained, restored, or deleted as needed.

Access Control: Policies and RBAC

Azure Key Vault supports two models for access control:

1. Access Policies

- Define which operations an identity can perform (get, list, set, delete).

- Managed at the Key Vault level.

- Ideal for application access and fine-grained control.

```
az keyvault set-policy \
  --name mykeyvault123 \
  --object-id <principal-object-id> \
  --secret-permissions get list set
```

2. Azure RBAC

- Uses Azure role assignments (Key Vault Secrets User, Key Vault Administrator, etc.).

- Managed at the resource or subscription level.

- Better for large-scale, centralized access control.

You can switch between models, but only one can be active at a time.

Managed Identities and Key Vault Integration

Azure services such as App Service, Functions, AKS, and VMs can be assigned managed identities. These identities can be granted access to Key Vault.

Enable Managed Identity (App Service)

1. Go to **App Service > Identity**

2. Enable **System-assigned managed identity**

3. Note the **Object ID**

Grant Access to Key Vault

```
az keyvault set-policy \
  --name mykeyvault123 \
  --object-id <object-id> \
  --secret-permissions get
```

Access from Code (C#)

```
var client = new SecretClient(new
Uri("https://mykeyvault123.vault.azure.net/"), new
DefaultAzureCredential());
KeyVaultSecret secret = await
client.GetSecretAsync("DbConnectionString");
```

```
string value = secret.Value;
```

DefaultAzureCredential handles managed identity, CLI logins, and Visual Studio authentication out of the box.

Key Vault in App Configuration

Instead of retrieving secrets programmatically, you can link Key Vault to **App Configuration** and reference secrets directly in your application settings.

Example (App Service Settings):
```
@Microsoft.KeyVault(SecretUri=https://mykeyvault123.vault.azure.net/
secrets/DbConnectionString/...)
```

This allows seamless use of secrets without writing retrieval logic in the application.

Secure Access with Private Endpoints

To prevent access over the public internet, enable **Private Endpoints** for your Key Vault:

1. Go to **Networking > Private Endpoint connections**

2. Click **+ Private Endpoint**

3. Choose a VNet and subnet

This limits access to resources within your virtual network.

Secret Lifecycle Management

Expiration and Automatic Rotation

You can set expiration dates and enable automated renewal with Key Vault certificates (integrated with DigiCert, GlobalSign, etc.).

For secrets and keys:

- Monitor expiration dates

- Use **Azure Automation** or **Logic Apps** for custom renewal scripts

- Tag versions for tracking rotation history

Soft Delete and Purge Protection

Key Vault protects against accidental or malicious deletion:

- **Soft delete** retains deleted items for 90 days

- **Purge protection** prevents permanent deletion

Enable via:

```
az keyvault update \
  --name mykeyvault123 \
  --enable-soft-delete true \
  --enable-purge-protection true
```

Auditing and Monitoring

Track all access and changes to your secrets using:

- **Azure Monitor**

- **Activity Logs**

- **Diagnostic Settings** (send logs to Log Analytics or Event Hub)

Example Log Analytics query:

```
AzureDiagnostics
| where ResourceType == "VAULTS"
| where OperationName contains "SecretGet"
| project TimeGenerated, CallerIpAddress, Identity, OperationName
```

Using Key Vault with Containers and Kubernetes

In containerized applications, avoid passing secrets as environment variables or config files.

AKS Integration

Use **AAD Pod Identity** or **CSI Secrets Store Driver** to mount secrets directly into pods:

```
volumeMounts:
  - name: secrets-store-inline
    mountPath: "/mnt/secrets-store"
    readOnly: true

volumes:
  - name: secrets-store-inline
    csi:
      driver: secrets-store.csi.k8s.io
      readOnly: true
      volumeAttributes:
        secretProviderClass: "azure-kv-provider"
```

Mounts secrets as files inside the container, reducing risk of exposure.

Key Vault and Encryption

Azure Key Vault allows you to manage your own **Customer-Managed Keys (CMK)** for services like:

- Azure Storage
- Azure SQL Database
- Azure Cosmos DB
- Azure Data Lake

These keys are stored in Key Vault and linked to services, enabling encryption at rest with full control.

```
az keyvault key create --name "myencryptionkey" --vault-name
mykeyvault123 --protection software
```

Linking a CMK ensures compliance with regulatory and data sovereignty requirements.

Best Practices

- Use **managed identities** for secure, keyless access to secrets

- Restrict access using **least privilege principle**

- Use **Private Endpoints** to eliminate public exposure

- Enable **soft delete** and **purge protection** to prevent data loss

- Rotate secrets regularly and monitor for expiry

- Never store secrets in environment variables or source code

- Centralize secret storage for all applications and environments

- Use **RBAC** for scalable access control when managing multiple vaults

Summary

Azure Key Vault is a critical component of a secure, compliant, and scalable cloud architecture. It provides a central place to manage secrets, keys, and certificates—eliminating the risks of hardcoded secrets and manual key management. With tight integration into Azure services, built-in support for automation, and robust access control, it enables developers and DevOps teams to build safer applications without sacrificing agility or productivity.

Key Takeaways:

- Centralized storage for secrets, keys, and certificates

- Fine-grained access control via policies or Azure RBAC

- Seamless integration with Azure services and managed identities

- Support for versioning, soft delete, and purge protection

- Secure key and secret delivery to applications and containers

- Best practices help reduce exposure and improve resilience

In the next section, we'll examine strategies for **load balancing and auto-scaling** applications in Azure, ensuring your solutions can handle production traffic with optimal performance and cost-efficiency.

Load Balancing and Auto-Scaling

Building scalable and highly available cloud-native applications is not just about writing performant code—it also requires a solid infrastructure strategy that can dynamically respond to changes in load and usage patterns. In Azure, achieving this elasticity involves a combination of **load balancing** and **auto-scaling** techniques that ensure your applications remain responsive, resilient, and cost-effective under varying workloads.

This section delves deep into Azure's load balancing and auto-scaling capabilities, covering essential services such as **Azure Load Balancer**, **Application Gateway**, **Traffic Manager**, **Front Door**, and **Virtual Machine Scale Sets (VMSS)**. We'll also explore how auto-scaling works across **App Services**, **AKS**, **Azure Functions**, and **container-based deployments**, along with best practices for monitoring and optimization.

Understanding Load Balancing

Load balancing is the distribution of incoming network traffic across multiple backend resources to ensure no single resource is overwhelmed. Azure provides various load balancing solutions depending on the scenario and application layer.

Types of Load Balancing in Azure

Service	Layer	Best Use Case
Azure Load Balancer	Layer 4 (TCP/UDP)	High-performance load balancing for VMs, AKS
Azure Application Gateway	Layer 7 (HTTP/HTTPS)	Application-level routing with WAF and SSL
Azure Traffic Manager	DNS-based	Geographic traffic distribution
Azure Front Door	Layer 7	Global app acceleration, SSL offloading, CDN

Azure Load Balancer

Azure Load Balancer is a high-throughput Layer 4 load balancer that distributes TCP/UDP traffic across VMs in a backend pool.

Key Features

- Supports inbound and outbound traffic
- Configurable health probes

- Availability zones and zone redundancy

- Integration with Virtual Machine Scale Sets (VMSS)

Basic Setup (CLI)

```
az network lb create \
  --resource-group MyRG \
  --name MyLoadBalancer \
  --frontend-ip-name MyFrontEnd \
  --backend-pool-name MyBackEndPool \
  --sku Standard \
  --public-ip-address myPublicIP
```

Attach VMs to the backend pool and configure health probes.

Azure Application Gateway

Application Gateway is a Layer 7 load balancer that enables advanced routing features, SSL termination, and Web Application Firewall (WAF).

Key Capabilities

- URL-based routing

- SSL offloading

- Cookie-based session affinity

- WAF with OWASP rulesets

- Autoscaling SKU available

Example Use Cases

- Route `/api/*` to backend API pool and `/images/*` to CDN

- Terminate HTTPS at the gateway, re-encrypt to backend

Deploy with WAF Enabled

```
az network application-gateway create \
  --name MyAppGateway \
```

```
--location eastus \
--resource-group MyRG \
--capacity 2 \
--sku WAF_v2 \
--http-settings-cookie-based-affinity Enabled \
--frontend-port 443 \
--ssl-cert-name mySSL \
--public-ip-address myAppGatewayIP
```

Azure Traffic Manager

Traffic Manager uses DNS to direct client requests based on routing policies.

Routing Methods

- **Priority**: Failover to backup endpoints

- **Weighted**: Load based on weights

- **Geographic**: Region-based routing

- **Latency**: Closest based on network latency

- **Multi-value**: Return multiple healthy endpoints

Ideal for disaster recovery, global distribution, and region-specific routing.

Azure Front Door

Front Door provides global HTTP(S) load balancing and acceleration.

Key Features

- Global Anycast IP

- Smart routing to closest backend

- SSL offloading and custom domains

- URL-based routing and rewriting

- Caching and compression

Use Front Door for low-latency, high-throughput global applications.

Auto-Scaling: The Elastic Cloud

Auto-scaling refers to the dynamic allocation or deallocation of resources based on load, time, or custom metrics.

Benefits

- Reduces over-provisioning

- Optimizes cost and performance

- Improves fault tolerance and redundancy

App Service Auto-Scaling

Azure App Service can scale automatically based on predefined rules.

Scale Conditions

- CPU usage

- Memory usage

- HTTP queue length

- Custom metrics (via Application Insights)

Configure Auto-Scale (CLI)

```
az monitor autoscale create \
  --resource-group MyRG \
  --resource MyWebApp \
  --resource-type Microsoft.Web/sites \
  --name autoscale-settings \
  --min-count 1 \
  --max-count 5 \
  --count 2
```

Add rules:

```
az monitor autoscale rule create \
  --resource-group MyRG \
  --autoscale-name autoscale-settings \
  --condition "CpuPercentage > 70 avg 5m" \
  --scale out 1
```

Azure Kubernetes Service (AKS) Scaling

Cluster Autoscaler

- Automatically adjusts node pool size

- Triggered by pending pods or underutilized nodes

Enable in ARM template or CLI:

```
az aks update \
  --name myAKSCluster \
  --resource-group MyRG \
  --enable-cluster-autoscaler \
  --min-count 1 \
  --max-count 5
```

Horizontal Pod Autoscaler (HPA)

Scales pod replicas based on CPU, memory, or custom metrics.

```
kubectl autoscale deployment myapp --cpu-percent=70 --min=1 --max=10
```

Requires metrics server installed in the cluster.

Azure Functions Auto-Scaling

Azure Functions scale automatically in the **Consumption Plan** and **Premium Plan**.

Consumption Plan

- Scales based on event volume (HTTP, queue, etc.)

- Billed per execution

- Ideal for bursty workloads

Premium Plan

- Pre-warmed instances

- More predictable latency

- VNET integration and longer timeouts

No configuration needed—Azure handles scaling based on trigger load.

Virtual Machine Scale Sets (VMSS)

VMSS lets you deploy and manage a set of auto-scaling VMs.

Features

- Uniform or flexible orchestration

- Load balancing integration

- Rolling upgrades and health probes

- Image-based or custom VM images

Create a Scale Set

```
az vmss create \
  --resource-group MyRG \
  --name MyScaleSet \
  --image UbuntuLTS \
  --upgrade-policy-mode automatic \
  --admin-username azureuser \
  --generate-ssh-keys
```

Add Auto-Scale Rules

```
az monitor autoscale create \
  --resource-group MyRG \
  --resource MyScaleSet \
  --resource-type Microsoft.Compute/virtualMachineScaleSets \
  --min-count 2 \
```

```
--max-count 10 \
--count 2
```

Monitoring and Observability

Use **Azure Monitor**, **Log Analytics**, and **Application Insights** to track:

- CPU and memory usage

- HTTP request count and response time

- Throttling or 429s

- Custom metrics and events

Example custom metric for scale:

```
az monitor metrics alert create \
  --name HighRequestRate \
  --resource MyWebApp \
  --condition "requests/count > 1000 avg 5m" \
  --action email alert@example.com
```

Best Practices

- Use **Application Gateway** for L7 traffic and WAF protection

- Use **Front Door** or **Traffic Manager** for global apps

- Combine **VMSS** with **Azure Load Balancer** for compute-intensive workloads

- Use **HPA** and **Cluster Autoscaler** in AKS for app and infra scaling

- Prefer **serverless** for event-driven or spiky workloads

- Monitor with **custom metrics** for precise scaling

- Set **cool-down periods** to prevent scale flapping

- Always test scale-in scenarios to ensure session and data integrity

Summary

Azure provides a rich toolbox of services for load balancing and auto-scaling, empowering developers and architects to build resilient, high-performance, and cost-optimized applications. By selecting the right combination of services—based on application architecture, workload patterns, and business requirements—you can ensure consistent availability and performance at any scale.

Key Takeaways:

- Use **Azure Load Balancer** for low-latency Layer 4 load distribution

- Leverage **Application Gateway** for SSL, routing, and WAF

- Use **Traffic Manager** and **Front Door** for geo-distribution

- Implement **auto-scaling** in App Service, AKS, VMSS, and Functions

- Monitor usage and performance to inform scaling decisions

- Align scale strategies with deployment models and SLAs

In the next section, we'll explore **monitoring and diagnostics with Azure Monitor**, which provides essential visibility into your application's health, performance, and operational metrics across all Azure services.

Monitoring and Diagnostics with Azure Monitor

Monitoring is a critical aspect of building, operating, and maintaining secure and performant applications in the cloud. Without adequate observability, it's impossible to know whether your applications are functioning correctly, how they're performing, or whether they're about to fail. Azure Monitor is Microsoft's unified monitoring service that collects, analyzes, and acts on telemetry from your cloud and on-premises environments.

This section provides an in-depth look into Azure Monitor and related services like **Application Insights**, **Log Analytics**, **Diagnostic Settings**, and **Alerts**. We'll cover how to instrument your applications, set up dashboards and alerts, debug performance issues, and integrate monitoring into your CI/CD and DevOps pipelines.

What is Azure Monitor?

Azure Monitor is a full-stack observability platform that provides insights into the availability, performance, and usage of applications, infrastructure, and network resources hosted in Azure, on-premises, or in other clouds.

It is composed of several interconnected services:

- **Metrics**: Real-time numerical data (CPU usage, memory, requests/sec)

- **Logs**: Structured and unstructured data (diagnostics, custom logs)

- **Application Insights**: Deep application performance monitoring (APM)

- **Log Analytics**: Query engine and workspace for log data

- **Alerts**: Trigger actions based on metrics and logs

- **Workbooks**: Custom visualizations and reports

- **Insights**: Prebuilt monitoring for Azure services (VMs, Containers, Databases)

Instrumenting Applications with Application Insights

Application Insights provides performance monitoring, error detection, and usage analytics for web applications and services.

Key Capabilities

- Distributed tracing

- Exception logging

- Dependency tracking (SQL, HTTP calls, etc.)

- Live metrics

- Custom telemetry and events

Adding Application Insights to a .NET App

1. Install the SDK:

```
dotnet add package Microsoft.ApplicationInsights.AspNetCore
```

2. Configure `Program.cs`:

```
builder.Services.AddApplicationInsightsTelemetry();
```

3. Set the instrumentation key in `appsettings.json`:

```json
{
  "ApplicationInsights": {
    "InstrumentationKey": "your-instrumentation-key"
  }
}
```

Azure App Services can auto-inject Application Insights without code changes.

Tracking Custom Events

```
telemetryClient.TrackEvent("UserLoggedIn", new Dictionary<string,
string> {
  { "UserId", userId }
});
```

Azure Monitor Metrics

Azure Monitor automatically collects standard metrics for all Azure resources.

Examples:

- CPU, memory, and disk usage

- HTTP request rate and failure count (App Services)

- Queue length (Service Bus)

- DTU usage (Azure SQL)

You can view metrics via:

- Azure Portal (Metrics explorer)

- Azure CLI

- REST API

- Dashboards and Workbooks

CLI Example

```
az monitor metrics list \
  --resource
"/subscriptions/{id}/resourceGroups/{group}/providers/Microsoft.Web/
sites/{app}" \
  --metric "Requests"
```

Log Analytics and the Kusto Query Language (KQL)

Log Analytics allows you to query telemetry data using **Kusto Query Language (KQL)**.

Creating a Log Analytics Workspace

```
az monitor log-analytics workspace create \
  --resource-group MyRG \
  --workspace-name MyWorkspace
```

Sample Queries

```
AppRequests
| where timestamp > ago(1h)
| summarize count() by resultCode

AzureDiagnostics
| where ResourceType == "APPLICATIONGATEWAYS"
| where operationName == "ApplicationGatewayAccess"
| summarize count() by httpStatusCode
```

KQL is highly expressive and supports filtering, joins, aggregations, and time series functions.

Diagnostic Settings

Enable **diagnostic settings** to send logs and metrics to:

- Log Analytics

- Event Hubs

- Azure Storage (archival)

CLI Example

```
az monitor diagnostic-settings create \
  --name "app-diagnostics" \
  --resource
"/subscriptions/xxx/resourceGroups/xxx/providers/Microsoft.Web/sites
/mywebapp" \
  --workspace MyWorkspaceId \
  --logs '[{"category": "AppServiceHTTPLogs", "enabled": true}]'
```

Enable diagnostic logs for services like:

- App Services

- Key Vault

- Application Gateway

- Cosmos DB

- Azure SQL

Setting Up Alerts

Azure Monitor supports metric- and log-based alerts.

Types of Alerts

- **Metric alerts**: Triggered by metrics (e.g., CPU > 80%)

- **Log alerts**: Based on KQL query results

- **Activity log alerts**: Triggered by Azure platform events (e.g., VM stopped)

- **Smart detection**: AI-based anomaly detection

Creating a Metric Alert (CLI)

```
az monitor metrics alert create \
```

```
  --name "HighCPUAlert" \
  --resource
"/subscriptions/xxx/resourceGroups/xxx/providers/Microsoft.Compute/v
irtualMachines/myvm" \
  --condition "Percentage CPU > 80" \
  --window-size 5m \
  --evaluation-frequency 1m \
  --action-group myAlertGroup
```

Alerts can trigger:

- Email or SMS notifications

- Webhooks

- Logic Apps or Azure Functions

- ITSM tools like ServiceNow

Workbooks: Visual Dashboards

Azure Monitor Workbooks provide rich, interactive dashboards and reports built on metrics and logs.

Use Cases

- DevOps and operational dashboards

- SLA tracking

- User behavior analysis

- API response time monitoring

Workbooks are highly customizable with charts, tables, metrics, and KQL queries. They can be parameterized and shared with teams.

Integration with DevOps and CI/CD

Monitoring should be part of your DevOps lifecycle.

GitHub Actions

Push logs and events to Application Insights on deployment:

```
- name: Send deployment event
  run: |
    curl -X POST "https://dc.services.visualstudio.com/v2/track" \
      -H "Content-Type: application/json" \
      -d '{
        "name": "Microsoft.ApplicationInsights.Deployment",
        "time": "'$(date -Iseconds)'",
        "iKey": "${{ secrets.APPINSIGHTS_KEY }}",
        "data": {
          "deploymentSource": "GitHub Actions",
          "deploymentId": "${{ github.run_id }}"
        }
      }'
```

Azure DevOps

- Add **deployment markers** to logs

- Use alerts to **pause pipelines** or **trigger rollbacks**

- Automatically generate dashboards for each environment

Distributed Tracing

For microservices and distributed apps, use **Application Map** in Application Insights:

- Visualizes service-to-service communication

- Shows failure hotspots

- Tracks performance bottlenecks

Enable distributed tracing by propagating context headers (e.g., `Request-Id`, `Correlation-Context`) between services.

For example, in .NET:

```
services.AddHttpClient()
```

```
.AddHttpMessageHandler(() => new DependencyTrackingHandler());
```

Monitoring Containers and AKS

Azure Monitor supports deep insights into Kubernetes clusters via **Container Insights**.

Features

- CPU and memory per container

- Pod restart counts

- Node health

- Live logs and metrics

Install monitoring agent via Azure CLI or enable in the portal during AKS creation.

View container performance with:

```
az aks enable-addons --addons monitoring --name myAKS --resource-
group MyRG
```

Cost Optimization and Monitoring

Use Azure Monitor to:

- Track resource usage patterns

- Identify idle services

- Detect memory leaks and slow queries

- Monitor cost spikes and anomalies

Query costs and usage with **Cost Management + Billing** or integrate with Log Analytics for deeper insights.

Best Practices

- **Centralize logs** with Log Analytics

- **Tag resources** to organize and filter logs by project, team, or environment

- Enable **retention policies** for cost-effective storage

- Use **alerts** proactively to detect issues before users do

- Build **dashboards** for real-time operational visibility

- Implement **application tracing** across microservices

- Automate **incident creation** and escalation workflows

- Align metrics with **SLAs and SLOs**

Summary

Monitoring and diagnostics are not optional in modern application development—they are essential for ensuring reliability, scalability, and customer trust. Azure Monitor and its suite of tools enable developers, DevOps engineers, and administrators to gain deep insight into applications and infrastructure, respond to incidents quickly, and continuously improve system performance.

Key Takeaways:

- **Application Insights** enables end-to-end application monitoring

- **Log Analytics** provides powerful log querying with KQL

- **Diagnostic Settings** extend telemetry to external systems

- **Azure Alerts** provide real-time notifications and auto-remediation

- **Workbooks** help visualize operational and business KPIs

- **Distributed tracing** supports microservices troubleshooting

- Use monitoring data to drive **optimization and scaling decisions**

In the next chapter, we will explore advanced development scenarios, including containers, AI integration, and serverless orchestration—unlocking even more power from the Azure platform.

Chapter 6: Advanced Development Scenarios

Using Azure Kubernetes Service (AKS)

As modern application architectures continue to evolve, containers have become a foundational technology for building scalable, portable, and consistent environments. Kubernetes has emerged as the de facto standard for container orchestration, offering powerful capabilities for managing distributed, containerized applications at scale. Azure Kubernetes Service (AKS) brings the power of Kubernetes to Azure with a managed, enterprise-grade platform designed for high availability, scalability, and developer productivity.

In this section, we'll explore AKS in detail: understanding its architecture, setting up clusters, deploying applications, integrating with CI/CD pipelines, scaling workloads, securing clusters, monitoring, and following best practices for production readiness.

What is Azure Kubernetes Service (AKS)?

AKS is a **managed Kubernetes** service that reduces the operational complexity of running Kubernetes. Microsoft handles critical tasks such as:

- Master node management

- Patching and upgrades

- Integration with Azure networking, monitoring, and identity

- Autoscaling infrastructure and workloads

This allows developers to focus on building applications while Azure takes care of the Kubernetes control plane.

Key Features of AKS

- **Managed Kubernetes Control Plane** (free of charge)

- **Automatic Node Scaling**

- **Integrated Monitoring with Azure Monitor**

- **Azure AD Integration**

- **Support for Windows and Linux Containers**

- **Private Clusters**

- **Integration with Dev Spaces, GitOps, and Azure Arc**

Core Components of AKS

- **Node Pools**: Sets of virtual machines (VMs) that run containerized applications.

- **Pods**: Smallest deployable units in Kubernetes; encapsulate one or more containers.

- **Deployments**: Describe how pods should be deployed and updated.

- **Services**: Provide network access to a set of pods.

- **Ingress Controllers**: Manage external access and routing to services.

Creating an AKS Cluster

You can create a cluster via the Azure Portal, Azure CLI, Bicep, or Terraform. Below is a sample using the Azure CLI.

CLI Example

```
az aks create \
  --resource-group MyResourceGroup \
  --name MyAKSCluster \
  --node-count 3 \
  --enable-addons monitoring \
  --enable-managed-identity \
  --generate-ssh-keys
```

Get Credentials

```
az aks get-credentials \
  --resource-group MyResourceGroup \
  --name MyAKSCluster
```

Now you can use `kubectl` to manage your cluster.

Deploying Your First Application

A simple example to deploy a containerized web app:

Deployment YAML (`deployment.yaml`)

```yaml
apiVersion: apps/v1
kind: Deployment
metadata:
  name: webapp-deployment
spec:
  replicas: 3
  selector:
    matchLabels:
      app: webapp
  template:
    metadata:
      labels:
        app: webapp
    spec:
      containers:
      - name: webapp
        image: nginx
        ports:
        - containerPort: 80
```

Service YAML (`service.yaml`)

```yaml
apiVersion: v1
kind: Service
metadata:
  name: webapp-service
spec:
  type: LoadBalancer
  selector:
    app: webapp
  ports:
  - port: 80
    targetPort: 80
```

Apply Configurations

```
kubectl apply -f deployment.yaml
kubectl apply -f service.yaml
```

Access your app using the external IP from the service.

Scaling Workloads

Horizontal Pod Autoscaler (HPA)

Automatically adjust the number of pods based on CPU usage or custom metrics.

```
kubectl autoscale deployment webapp-deployment --cpu-percent=70 --min=1 --max=10
```

Ensure that the metrics server is installed in the cluster.

Cluster Autoscaler

Adjusts the number of nodes in a node pool based on pending pods.

Enable with:

```
az aks update \
  --resource-group MyResourceGroup \
  --name MyAKSCluster \
  --enable-cluster-autoscaler \
  --min-count 1 \
  --max-count 5
```

Securing AKS Clusters

Security is vital for Kubernetes workloads. AKS offers multiple layers of security:

Azure Active Directory Integration

Use Azure AD for RBAC within Kubernetes:

```
az aks create \
  --enable-aad \
  --aad-admin-group-object-ids <group-id> \
  ...
```

Network Policies

Control traffic between pods with network policy definitions.

Secrets Management

Use **Kubernetes Secrets** or integrate with **Azure Key Vault** via **CSI drivers**.

Example Secret:

```
apiVersion: v1
kind: Secret
metadata:
  name: mysecret
type: Opaque
data:
  username: YWRtaW4=    # base64 encoded
  password: MWYyZDFlMmU2N2Rm
```

Image Security

- Use **Azure Container Registry (ACR)**
- Enable **content scanning**
- Use **Pod Security Policies** or **OPA/Gatekeeper** for compliance

---

Monitoring and Logging

Azure Monitor for Containers

Provides visibility into:

- Node and pod resource usage
- Container logs and events
- Failed deployments and pod restarts

Enable during AKS creation:

```
az aks enable-addons \
```

```
--addons monitoring \
--name MyAKSCluster \
--resource-group MyResourceGroup
```

Use **Log Analytics** for advanced queries:

```
KubePodInventory
| summarize count() by ContainerStatus
```

Application Insights

Use Application Insights SDK in containerized applications for:

- Request tracing

- Dependency tracking

- Custom telemetry

Ingress Controllers and TLS

Use **NGINX** or **AGIC (Application Gateway Ingress Controller)** for external access.

Install NGINX Ingress
```
helm repo add ingress-nginx https://kubernetes.github.io/ingress-nginx
helm install ingress ingress-nginx/ingress-nginx
```

Sample Ingress YAML
```
apiVersion: networking.k8s.io/v1
kind: Ingress
metadata:
  name: webapp-ingress
  annotations:
    nginx.ingress.kubernetes.io/rewrite-target: /
spec:
  rules:
  - host: webapp.example.com
    http:
      paths:
```

```
    - path: /
      pathType: Prefix
      backend:
        service:
          name: webapp-service
          port:
            number: 80
```

Configure DNS and TLS for secure, domain-based routing.

CI/CD Integration

Use **Azure DevOps** or **GitHub Actions** to automate deployment.

Sample GitHub Workflow

```
name: Deploy to AKS

on:
  push:
    branches:
      - main

jobs:
  deploy:
    runs-on: ubuntu-latest
    steps:
      - uses: actions/checkout@v2
      - uses: Azure/aks-set-context@v1
        with:
          creds: ${{ secrets.AZURE_CREDENTIALS }}
          cluster-name: MyAKSCluster
          resource-group: MyResourceGroup
      - run: kubectl apply -f k8s/
```

Best Practices

- Use **managed identities** to avoid hardcoded credentials

- Monitor resource limits and requests per container

- Use **liveness** and **readiness probes** to ensure app health

- Implement **PodDisruptionBudgets** for controlled updates

- Regularly **rotate secrets** and certificates

- Limit cluster access via **Network Security Groups (NSGs)**

- Use **Azure Policy for AKS** to enforce governance

- Secure images using **Azure Defender for Containers**

Summary

Azure Kubernetes Service empowers developers and DevOps teams to deploy and manage containerized applications with scalability, reliability, and agility. With full integration into the Azure ecosystem, AKS enables the adoption of microservices, DevSecOps, and modern CI/CD pipelines while abstracting the complexity of managing Kubernetes infrastructure.

Key Takeaways:

- AKS simplifies Kubernetes setup and operations on Azure

- Use deployments, services, and ingress to run scalable apps

- Secure clusters with Azure AD, network policies, and Key Vault

- Scale dynamically using HPA and Cluster Autoscaler

- Integrate with Azure Monitor and Application Insights for observability

- Automate deployments with GitHub Actions or Azure DevOps

In the next section, we will explore how to harness the power of **AI and Machine Learning** in your applications using Azure's ecosystem of intelligent services.

AI and Machine Learning Integration

Artificial Intelligence (AI) and Machine Learning (ML) are rapidly transforming modern application development by enabling systems to learn from data, adapt to new information, and make decisions with minimal human intervention. Azure offers a comprehensive suite of

AI and ML tools that make it easier for developers to integrate intelligent capabilities into their applications—without necessarily being data science experts.

This section explores the full breadth of AI and ML capabilities in Azure, including pre-built cognitive services, custom model training using Azure Machine Learning, integration with application code, deployment strategies, automation, and best practices. Whether you're building a chatbot, image recognition pipeline, recommendation engine, or fraud detection system, Azure provides the infrastructure and tools you need to deliver intelligent applications at scale.

The Azure AI Platform Overview

Azure offers a wide spectrum of AI and ML tools grouped into three main layers:

1. **Pre-built AI Services (Cognitive Services)**

   o Ready-to-use APIs for vision, speech, language, and decision-making

2. **Custom AI (Azure Machine Learning)**

   o Build, train, and deploy custom machine learning models

3. **Infrastructure and Tooling**

   o Scalable compute, data storage, pipelines, MLOps

Azure Cognitive Services

Azure Cognitive Services are a collection of AI services that provide pre-trained models via simple REST APIs and SDKs.

Key Categories

Category	Capabilities
Vision	Image analysis, OCR, face detection, video indexing
Speech	Speech-to-text, text-to-speech, translation
Language	Text analytics, sentiment analysis, entity recognition

| Decision | Personalizer, Anomaly Detector, Content Moderator |
| OpenAI | Natural language understanding and generation (GPT models) |

Example: Using Computer Vision API

1. Create a Computer Vision resource in Azure

2. Use the endpoint and key to analyze an image

```
import requests

endpoint =
"https://<region>.api.cognitive.microsoft.com/vision/v3.2/analyze"
subscription_key = "<your-key>"

params = {'visualFeatures': 'Categories,Description,Color'}
headers = {'Ocp-Apim-Subscription-Key': subscription_key,
           'Content-Type': 'application/json'}
data = {'url': 'https://example.com/image.jpg'}

response = requests.post(endpoint, headers=headers, params=params,
json=data)
print(response.json())
```

You can use SDKs for Python, Java, .NET, and JavaScript for ease of integration.

Azure OpenAI Service

Azure OpenAI brings large language models like GPT-4, Codex, and DALL·E to Azure, enabling advanced language understanding and generation.

Use Cases

- Chatbots and conversational agents

- Code completion and generation

- Text summarization and classification

- Creative content generation

Sample API Call

```python
import openai

openai.api_type = "azure"
openai.api_base = "https://<your-endpoint>.openai.azure.com/"
openai.api_key = "<your-api-key>"
openai.api_version = "2023-03-15-preview"

response = openai.ChatCompletion.create(
    engine="gpt-4",
    messages=[{"role": "user", "content": "Explain quantum computing"}]
)
print(response['choices'][0]['message']['content'])
```

Azure ensures enterprise-grade security, scalability, and compliance for AI workloads using OpenAI models.

Azure Machine Learning (Azure ML)

For custom models, **Azure ML** provides a full platform for ML model lifecycle management: data preparation, training, deployment, and monitoring.

Key Components

- **Workspaces**: Central management for datasets, models, and experiments

- **Compute Targets**: On-demand scalable VMs or clusters

- **Pipelines**: Reusable workflows for training and deployment

- **Experiments**: Track runs and compare metrics

- **Endpoints**: Real-time and batch inference

Creating a Workspace (CLI)

```
az ml workspace create --name mymlworkspace --resource-group MyRG
```

Training a Model (Python SDK)

```python
from azureml.core import Workspace, Experiment, ScriptRunConfig,
Environment

ws = Workspace.from_config()
exp = Experiment(workspace=ws, name='myexperiment')

env = Environment.from_conda_specification(name='myenv',
file_path='env.yml')
src = ScriptRunConfig(source_directory='scripts', script='train.py',
environment=env)

run = exp.submit(src)
run.wait_for_completion(show_output=True)
```

Deploying a Model

```python
from azureml.core.model import Model
from azureml.core.webservice import AciWebservice, Webservice
from azureml.core.model import InferenceConfig

model = Model.register(workspace=ws, model_name='my_model',
model_path='outputs/model.pkl')
inference_config = InferenceConfig(entry_script="score.py",
environment=env)
deployment_config = AciWebservice.deploy_configuration(cpu_cores=1,
memory_gb=1)

service = Model.deploy(workspace=ws, name="myservice",
models=[model],
                        inference_config=inference_config,
deployment_config=deployment_config)
service.wait_for_deployment(show_output=True)
```

Your model is now available via a REST endpoint.

MLOps with Azure

MLOps applies DevOps principles to the ML lifecycle, enabling:

- Reproducible training

- Automated deployments

- Model versioning

- Continuous monitoring and retraining

Tools for MLOps

- **Azure DevOps** or **GitHub Actions** for CI/CD

- **Azure Machine Learning Pipelines**

- **Model Registry**

- **MLflow** support for logging experiments

- **Azure Monitor** for inference logging and alerting

You can define a full ML pipeline from data ingestion to deployment in code or via the Azure ML designer.

Real-Time vs. Batch Inference

Type	Characteristics
Real-Time	Fast response (REST APIs), used in apps and chatbots
Batch	Periodic processing of large datasets

Azure ML supports both via **online endpoints** (ACI/AKS) and **batch endpoints** (compute clusters or data factories).

Integrating AI in Applications

Use AI-powered services in:

Web Applications

- User personalization (via Personalizer)

- Text translation (via Translator)

- Image uploads with moderation (via Content Moderator)

- Dynamic product search (via Language Understanding)

Mobile Apps

- OCR and barcode scanning (via Vision API)

- Voice commands and transcription (via Speech SDK)

- On-device ML with ONNX Runtime and Azure Percept

Backend Systems

- Predictive maintenance

- Fraud detection

- Automated document processing (with Form Recognizer)

Cost and Optimization

AI and ML workloads can be cost-intensive. Consider:

- **Auto-shutdown** of idle compute clusters

- **Spot VMs** for non-critical training

- **Batch scoring** for cost-efficient inference

- **Scaling endpoints** based on demand

- Choosing appropriate **tiers** for Cognitive Services

Track usage via **Azure Cost Management** and set budgets and alerts.

Security and Governance

- Use **Azure Key Vault** for storing API keys and connection strings

- Apply **RBAC** and **role assignments** for access control

- Use **Private Endpoints** for data ingress/egress

- Enable **audit logs** and **network isolation** in workspaces

- Classify and label data for responsible AI and compliance

Responsible AI

Azure provides tools and guidance for ethical AI practices:

- **Fairlearn**: Bias and fairness analysis

- **InterpretML**: Explainable AI (SHAP, LIME)

- **Data Drift Detection**: Monitor model degradation

- **Confidential Computing**: Protect models and data at runtime

Azure's Responsible AI dashboard helps ensure transparency, accountability, and trust.

Best Practices

- Use pre-built Cognitive Services for rapid prototyping

- Train custom models with Azure ML only when needed

- Containerize models for portability (using MLflow or ONNX)

- Automate model retraining and redeployment with pipelines

- Monitor performance and drift continuously

- Use **telemetry** to understand model impact in production

- Secure training and inference endpoints

- Enable audit trails for data lineage and model provenance

Summary

Integrating AI and ML into applications no longer requires specialized infrastructure or deep data science expertise. Azure's powerful ecosystem makes it easy to build intelligent solutions—from drag-and-drop pipelines to cutting-edge language models—while maintaining security, governance, and scalability. Whether using pre-built services or training custom models, Azure enables developers to unlock the full potential of intelligent applications.

Key Takeaways:

- Use **Cognitive Services** and **OpenAI** for plug-and-play intelligence

- Build custom models using **Azure Machine Learning**

- Deploy models using real-time and batch inference endpoints

- Apply **MLOps** principles to automate and govern the ML lifecycle

- Monitor, optimize, and secure your AI workflows with built-in tools

In the next section, we'll explore how to build **event-driven architectures** using Azure services like Event Grid, Service Bus, and Event Hubs to enable loosely coupled, scalable, and reactive systems.

Event-Driven Architectures with Event Grid and Service Bus

As modern systems become more distributed and responsive, event-driven architectures (EDAs) offer a powerful pattern for building loosely coupled, scalable, and reactive applications. These architectures rely on events to trigger behavior across independent services, allowing components to operate autonomously and evolve independently. Azure supports event-driven architectures through services like **Event Grid**, **Service Bus**, and **Event Hubs**, each designed for specific messaging and event distribution scenarios.

This section dives into the principles of event-driven design, explains how to use Azure's eventing and messaging services, and illustrates patterns and use cases for building resilient and decoupled applications. We'll cover core concepts, service selection, integration, security, performance, and best practices.

What is Event-Driven Architecture?

Event-Driven Architecture is a software design pattern in which components communicate by publishing and subscribing to **events**, rather than calling each other directly.

Key Benefits

- **Loose coupling** between components

- **High scalability** due to asynchronous processing

- **Improved fault tolerance** and retry logic

- **Better maintainability** and extensibility

- **Real-time responsiveness**

Core Concepts

- **Event Producers**: Generate and emit events (e.g., app services, databases)

- **Event Consumers**: React to events and perform actions (e.g., functions, microservices)

- **Event Brokers**: Intermediate systems that route, filter, and deliver events (e.g., Event Grid, Service Bus)

Choosing the Right Azure Service

Feature	Event Grid	Service Bus	Event Hubs
Ideal for	Lightweight eventing	Enterprise messaging	Telemetry ingestion
Protocols	HTTP/HTTPS	AMQP, HTTP	AMQP, Kafka, HTTPS
Message durability	At-least-once	FIFO, Dead-letter queues	Streaming with offset
Message size	Up to 1 MB	Up to 1 MB	Up to 1 MB
Event routing	Yes (filters)	Limited	No

Advanced scenarios	Fan-out, webhooks	Order, transactions	Real-time analytics

Event Grid: Lightweight Event Routing

Azure Event Grid is a fully managed event routing service that enables building event-based applications by using a publish-subscribe model.

Key Features

- Native integration with Azure services (e.g., Blob Storage, Resource Groups)

- Push-based delivery (HTTP/S)

- Advanced filtering

- Dead-lettering

- Retry policies with exponential backoff

Supported Event Sources

- Azure Blob Storage

- Azure Resource Manager

- Azure Media Services

- Custom applications (via HTTP POST)

Supported Event Handlers

- Azure Functions

- Azure Logic Apps

- Azure WebHooks

- Azure Event Hubs

- Azure Automation

Sample: Subscribe to Blob Storage Events

```
az eventgrid event-subscription create \
  --name onBlobCreated \
  --source-resource-id
/subscriptions/xxxx/resourceGroups/xxxx/providers/Microsoft.Storage/
storageAccounts/mystorage \
  --endpoint https://myapp.azurewebsites.net/api/Notify
```

You can filter events using subject patterns and event types.

Service Bus: Enterprise Messaging

Azure Service Bus is a fully managed enterprise message broker that enables asynchronous communication between services and applications.

Key Features

- Queues and Topics for messaging

- Message ordering (FIFO)

- Duplicate detection

- Dead-letter queues

- Sessions for stateful messaging

- Scheduled and deferred messages

- Transaction support

Use Cases

- Decoupling services with queues

- Fan-out message processing with topics

- Implementing sagas and workflows

- Reliable message delivery

Sample: Send and Receive Messages (Python)

```python
from azure.servicebus import ServiceBusClient, ServiceBusMessage
```

```
connection_str = "<your-connection-string>"
queue_name = "myqueue"

with ServiceBusClient.from_connection_string(connection_str) as
client:
    sender = client.get_queue_sender(queue_name)
    with sender:
        sender.send_messages(ServiceBusMessage("Hello Azure!"))

    receiver = client.get_queue_receiver(queue_name)
    with receiver:
        for msg in receiver:
            print(str(msg))
            receiver.complete_message(msg)
```

Use sessions for grouped messages and ordered processing.

Event Hubs: Big Data Ingestion

Azure Event Hubs is a big data streaming platform and event ingestion service capable of receiving and processing millions of events per second.

Key Features

- High-throughput event ingestion

- Kafka-compatible endpoint

- Real-time and batch processing

- Offset and checkpoint tracking

- Integration with Azure Stream Analytics, Databricks, and HDInsight

Use Cases

- IoT telemetry ingestion

- Real-time analytics

- Log and metrics collection

- Live dashboarding

Sample: Ingest Data with Python

```
from azure.eventhub import EventHubProducerClient, EventData

producer = EventHubProducerClient.from_connection_string(
    conn_str="<your-connection-string>", eventhub_name="myeventhub")

event_data_batch = producer.create_batch()
event_data_batch.add(EventData('{"temperature": 25.3, "deviceId":
"sensor1"}'))
producer.send_batch(event_data_batch)
```

Integration Patterns

Fan-Out Pattern

Use Event Grid to distribute a single event to multiple subscribers:

- File uploaded to Blob Storage

- Event Grid sends notification to:

  - Azure Function (process image)

  - Logic App (notify user)

  - Event Hub (log activity)

Queue-Based Load Leveling

Use Service Bus queues to absorb load spikes:

- Web API accepts orders and sends to queue

- Backend worker reads from queue and processes asynchronously

- Queue acts as a buffer during high load

Retry and Dead-Letter

- Event Grid retries with exponential backoff

- Service Bus provides dead-letter queues for undeliverable messages

- Implement logic to reprocess or alert on dead-letter events

Event Chaining and Workflows

Chain multiple services using events:

1. Order placed → Event sent to Event Grid

2. Event triggers Azure Function to process payment

3. If successful, another event triggers inventory update

4. Completion event triggers customer notification

Use **Event Grid Domains** for managing events across large, multi-tenant systems.

Monitoring and Diagnostics

- **Azure Monitor** for metrics and logs

- **Diagnostic settings** for delivery success/failure events

- **Log Analytics** for querying events

- **Application Insights** for tracing event flows

Sample KQL Query (Service Bus):

```
AzureDiagnostics
| where ResourceType == "SERVICEBUSNAMESPACES"
| where OperationName == "Send"
| summarize count() by bin(TimeGenerated, 1h), StatusCode
```

Use alerts to detect spikes in failed deliveries.

Security Considerations

- Use **Azure RBAC** to control access to event/messaging resources

- Enable **Managed Identities** for authentication

- Use **Private Endpoints** for secure communication

- Encrypt messages in transit and at rest

- Validate webhook requests with validation codes or secrets

Cost Optimization

- Choose the appropriate SKU (Basic, Standard, Premium) based on feature needs

- Aggregate events to reduce delivery costs

- Use batch processing for Event Hubs

- Monitor ingress/egress and scale accordingly

- Clean up unused subscriptions and queues

Best Practices

- Keep message payloads small (ideally < 64 KB for Service Bus)

- Use dead-letter queues for error handling and reprocessing

- Leverage **topic filters** to reduce unnecessary processing

- Implement idempotent consumers to handle duplicate messages

- Secure endpoints with validation tokens or OAuth

- Monitor health with end-to-end tracing

- Use **cloud-native patterns** like pub/sub and CQRS

Summary

Event-driven architecture enables systems to be more responsive, scalable, and loosely coupled—qualities that are vital for building cloud-native applications. Azure provides a powerful suite of eventing and messaging services that support a variety of use cases from simple notifications to high-volume telemetry ingestion and enterprise-grade asynchronous communication.

Key Takeaways:

- Use **Event Grid** for lightweight, reactive, event-driven scenarios

- Use **Service Bus** for reliable, ordered, and transactional messaging

- Use **Event Hubs** for large-scale telemetry and data ingestion

- Combine services for complex workflows and scalable designs

- Implement robust monitoring, retries, and security

- Follow best practices to ensure durability and cost efficiency

In the next section, we'll look at how to orchestrate complex business processes using **Azure Logic Apps**—a powerful tool for building no-code/low-code workflows that integrate with hundreds of services.

Azure Logic Apps and Workflow Automation

As modern cloud applications grow in complexity and scale, there's a growing need to automate business processes, integrate with diverse systems, and orchestrate workflows across services. Azure Logic Apps is a low-code/no-code integration platform designed to meet this need. It empowers developers and business users to build scalable, event-driven workflows that connect cloud and on-premises systems without writing extensive code.

This section explores how Azure Logic Apps works, its core components, integration capabilities, developer tooling, pricing, and real-world automation scenarios. We'll also dive into how Logic Apps compares with alternatives like Azure Functions and Power Automate, and how it fits within a broader enterprise architecture.

What is Azure Logic Apps?

Azure Logic Apps is a cloud-based service that enables you to automate workflows and integrate apps, data, services, and systems. You can use Logic Apps to:

- Build and orchestrate business processes

- Automate data flows across cloud services and APIs

- React to events in real-time

- Integrate legacy systems with cloud-based solutions

- Connect to enterprise systems like SAP, Oracle, and Dynamics 365

Logic Apps supports hundreds of prebuilt connectors and can be customized using code snippets, expressions, and Azure Functions.

Core Concepts

Workflow

A **workflow** is the central unit of automation. It is defined as a series of steps that execute based on triggers and conditions.

Trigger

A **trigger** starts a Logic App. Examples include:

- HTTP request

- New email in Outlook

- File uploaded to SharePoint or Blob Storage

- Schedule-based trigger (cron)

Actions

Actions are tasks executed in response to a trigger or preceding step. Examples include:

- Sending an email

- Calling an API

- Writing data to a database

- Starting a new workflow

Connectors

Connectors enable Logic Apps to integrate with services. They are available in four categories:

Type	Examples
Standard	HTTP, Azure Blob Storage, SQL Server
Premium	SAP, Oracle DB, IBM MQ
Custom	Your own REST APIs or OpenAPI definitions
Enterprise	B2B, EDIFACT, AS2, X12

Building a Workflow (Example)

Imagine automating a leave request approval system:

1. **Trigger**: Employee submits a request via Microsoft Forms

2. **Action**: Store form data in SharePoint

3. **Condition**: If days requested > 5, notify HR

4. **Action**: Send email to manager for approval

5. **Action**: Store approval result in SQL Database

6. **Action**: Send notification to employee

Each of these steps is configured visually in the Logic Apps Designer or defined as JSON in the Logic Apps code view.

Creating a Logic App

Azure Portal

1. Go to **Create a Resource > Logic App**

2. Choose **Consumption**, **Standard**, or **Workflow App** (for Functions-based hosting)

3. Define resource group, region, and name

4. Open **Logic App Designer**

5. Select a **trigger** (e.g., HTTP Request or Recurrence)

6. Add steps using **prebuilt connectors** or inline code

VS Code (Standard Logic Apps)

Logic Apps Standard supports local development using the Azure Logic Apps (Preview) extension.

```
func init mylogicapp --worker-runtime node
cd mylogicapp
func new --template "Logic App Workflow"
```

You can deploy workflows via Azure DevOps or GitHub Actions for CI/CD.

Common Integration Scenarios

File Processing Pipeline

- Trigger: Blob created in storage

- Actions:

    - Parse file contents

    - Validate data (e.g., with inline conditions or custom code)

    - Store valid rows in SQL Server

    - Move invalid data to a separate container

    - Notify team on failure

HR Onboarding Automation

- Trigger: New employee in HR system

- Actions:

    - Provision user in Azure AD

- o Create mailbox and Teams account

- o Add to internal groups

- o Send welcome email

- o Schedule orientation events

IoT Device Data Routing

- Trigger: Event Hub receives telemetry

- Actions:

  - o Analyze data using Azure Functions

  - o If thresholds exceeded, raise alert

  - o Store metrics in Cosmos DB

  - o Notify operator via Teams

Advanced Logic App Features

Expressions and Conditions

Use **Workflow Definition Language (WDL)** expressions to manipulate data.

```
"if": [
  {
    "equals": ["@triggerBody()['Status']", "Approved"]
  }
]
```

You can use @utcNow(), @concat(), @formatDateTime(), and more.

Looping and Parallel Execution

- **For Each**: Iterate over arrays or collections

- **Until**: Loop until a condition is met

- **Scopes**: Group steps for retry logic and error handling

- **Run After**: Define control flow dependencies

Error Handling and Retries

- Each action can be configured with:

  - Retry policy (e.g., exponential backoff)

  - Timeout

  - "Run After" conditions (e.g., run after failure)

- Use **Try/Catch** equivalent with **Scopes** and **Configure Run After**

Integration with Azure Services

Azure Service	Integration Approach
Azure Functions	Inline or connector-based function invocation
Cosmos DB	Insert or query documents with a connector
Event Grid	Trigger Logic App on event published
Service Bus	Trigger from queue or topic message
SQL Database	Read, insert, update records via connector
Azure Monitor	Trigger on metrics, logs, or alerts

You can chain Logic Apps with Event Grid or Functions to build complex workflows using micro-orchestration.

Security and Governance

- **Managed Identity**: Securely access Azure services

- **IP Restrictions and VNET Integration**: Isolate workflows

- **Azure Key Vault**: Store and retrieve secrets securely

- **Authentication**: Use OAuth2, API keys, or certificates

- **Auditing**: Enable diagnostic logs and send to Log Analytics

---

Monitoring and Troubleshooting

- **Run History**: View individual workflow executions

- **Diagnostics Logs**: Track success, failure, latency

- **Azure Monitor and Application Insights**: Track metrics and custom telemetry

- **Failure Alerts**: Use Logic Apps or Azure Alerts to respond to failures

You can use built-in visualizations or route data to Power BI for reporting.

CI/CD with Logic Apps

GitHub Actions Example

```
- uses: azure/login@v1
  with:
    creds: ${{ secrets.AZURE_CREDENTIALS }}

- uses: Azure/cli@v1
  with:
    inlineScript: |
      az logicapp deployment source config-zip \
        --name mylogicapp \
        --resource-group MyRG \
        --src logicapp.zip
```

Azure DevOps Pipelines

- Use **ARM templates** or **Bicep** for infrastructure

- Deploy workflows as part of release pipelines

- Store definitions in source control

Pricing Models

- **Consumption**: Pay per execution (great for infrequent workflows)

- **Standard**: Fixed compute cost, ideal for high-throughput apps

- **Integration Service Environment (ISE)**: For enterprise workloads needing VNET integration and isolation

Choose based on expected volume, performance needs, and integration requirements.

Comparison: Logic Apps vs. Functions vs. Power Automate

Feature	Logic Apps	Azure Functions	Power Automate
Coding Required	No (low-code)	Yes (full code)	No (GUI-based)
Ideal For	Integration workflows	Custom logic and services	Business users
Triggers	HTTP, Event Grid, etc.	HTTP, Timer, Event Grid	SharePoint, Outlook, etc.
CI/CD Support	Yes	Yes	Limited
Target Audience	Developers	Developers	Citizen developers

Best Practices

- Use **naming conventions** for workflows and resources

- Group actions in **scopes** for better readability

- Handle **errors and timeouts** with retry policies

- Use **Key Vault** for credentials, not plain-text parameters

- Enable **logging and diagnostics** from day one

- Modularize logic with **child Logic Apps**

- Apply **RBAC** for access control

- Secure endpoints with **IP restrictions and OAuth**

Summary

Azure Logic Apps simplifies workflow automation and systems integration by providing a visual designer, hundreds of prebuilt connectors, and robust tooling for enterprise workloads. Whether you're processing documents, orchestrating approvals, or reacting to real-time data, Logic Apps can help you deliver scalable, secure, and reliable workflows quickly.

Key Takeaways:

- Use Logic Apps for automating business processes and integrating systems

- Build event-driven workflows with triggers and actions

- Choose between Consumption, Standard, and ISE plans based on needs

- Monitor workflows with Azure Monitor, logs, and diagnostics

- Secure workflows with managed identity, Key Vault, and network isolation

- Integrate with DevOps pipelines for CI/CD and version control

In the next chapter, we'll explore **real-world use cases** and demonstrate how organizations leverage Azure to deliver robust, scalable, and cost-effective cloud solutions.

Chapter 7: Real-World Use Cases and Solutions

Building a SaaS Product on Azure

Software as a Service (SaaS) is a dominant delivery model in today's software economy. It allows vendors to provide applications over the internet without requiring users to install or manage software themselves. Building a successful SaaS product involves much more than developing an application; it requires careful architectural choices, secure multi-tenancy, scalable infrastructure, automated deployments, monitoring, and cost management. Azure offers a rich set of tools and services tailored to the needs of SaaS builders, whether targeting consumers, businesses, or enterprises.

In this section, we'll walk through how to build a robust SaaS product on Azure—from planning the architecture and selecting core services to implementing multi-tenant logic, automating onboarding, scaling dynamically, and ensuring operational excellence. We'll use examples to demonstrate key concepts and show how they tie together into a coherent SaaS platform.

SaaS Architecture Overview

A well-architected SaaS solution is designed to serve multiple customers (tenants) from a shared infrastructure while maintaining **data isolation**, **performance guarantees**, and **security**.

Key Architectural Patterns

1. **Single-Tenant Per Deployment**
   Each customer gets a dedicated instance (App Service, DB, etc.)

   - Pros: Strong isolation, easy customization

   - Cons: High cost, operational complexity

2. **Single Shared Deployment (Multi-Tenant)**
   All customers share a common app and database, with tenant-aware logic

   - Pros: Cost-efficient, scalable

   - Cons: More complex design and governance

3. **Hybrid (Pooled + Dedicated Services)**
   Share some resources (e.g., app), isolate others (e.g., DB)

○ Balanced cost, scalability, and control

For this chapter, we'll focus primarily on the **multi-tenant shared deployment model**, the most common in modern SaaS applications.

Key Azure Services for SaaS

Component	Azure Service
Compute	App Service, Azure Functions, AKS
Identity	Azure Active Directory B2C / Azure AD
Data Storage	Azure SQL Database, Cosmos DB, Blob
Message Queue	Azure Service Bus, Event Grid
Monitoring	Azure Monitor, Application Insights
Billing & Usage	Azure Cost Management + Custom Logic
Deployment	Azure DevOps, GitHub Actions

Identity and Access Control

Managing identities and controlling access is crucial in SaaS. Tenants must be isolated from each other, and users must be authenticated within the context of their tenant.

Azure AD B2C

Use **Azure Active Directory B2C** for customer-facing identity management:

- Self-service sign-up/sign-in

- Social and enterprise ID federation

- Custom branding and policies

{

```
  "signInAudience": "AzureADandPersonalMicrosoftAccount",
  "replyUrlsWithType": [
    {
      "url": "https://your-saas-app.com",
      "type": "Web"
    }
  ]
}
```

Claims-Based Authorization

Pass the tenant ID in JWT claims and enforce tenant-level access:

```
services.AddAuthorization(options =>
{
    options.AddPolicy("TenantScoped", policy =>
        policy.RequireClaim("tenant_id"));
});
```

Multi-Tenancy in Data Layer

Shared Database with Tenant ID Column

Design tables to include a TenantId column:

```
CREATE TABLE Orders (
    OrderId INT PRIMARY KEY,
    TenantId UNIQUEIDENTIFIER,
    ProductId INT,
    Quantity INT
);
```

Use filtered queries:

```
SELECT * FROM Orders WHERE TenantId = @TenantId
```

Data Isolation with Row-Level Security

SQL Server supports **Row-Level Security (RLS)** to enforce tenant data visibility:

```
CREATE FUNCTION fn_securitypredicate(@TenantId UNIQUEIDENTIFIER)
```

```
RETURNS TABLE
WITH SCHEMABINDING
AS
    RETURN SELECT 1 AS result WHERE @TenantId =
CAST(SESSION_CONTEXT(N'TenantId') AS UNIQUEIDENTIFIER);

CREATE SECURITY POLICY TenantSecurityPolicy
ADD FILTER PREDICATE fn_securitypredicate(TenantId) ON dbo.Orders,
ADD BLOCK PREDICATE fn_securitypredicate(TenantId) ON dbo.Orders
```

Set session context on app layer:

```
using (var conn = new SqlConnection(...)) {
    var cmd = conn.CreateCommand();
    cmd.CommandText = "EXEC sp_set_session_context @key=N'TenantId',
@value=@tenantId";
}
```

Onboarding New Tenants

Automating onboarding is critical for SaaS at scale.

1. Collect tenant info (e.g., company name, email) via web form

2. Generate subdomain or tenant ID

3. Provision tenant-specific resources:

   o Resource group (optional)

   o Database entry

   o User groups and roles

4. Send welcome email

Use **Azure Functions** or **Logic Apps** to automate these steps using workflows or ARM/Bicep templates.

Billing and Metering

Azure doesn't provide native tenant billing for custom apps. You'll need to implement:

- Usage tracking (API calls, data stored, compute time)

- Custom billing engine

- Integration with Stripe, Azure Marketplace, etc.

Track usage via:

- Azure Monitor Metrics

- Custom logs in Application Insights

- Event Grid hooks for metering triggers

CI/CD and Deployment Strategy

Use CI/CD pipelines to manage updates without downtime across tenants.

GitHub Actions Example

```
name: Deploy SaaS App

on:
  push:
    branches:
      - main

jobs:
  deploy:
    runs-on: ubuntu-latest
    steps:
      - uses: actions/checkout@v3
      - uses: azure/webapps-deploy@v2
        with:
          app-name: 'your-saas-app'
          publish-profile: ${{ secrets.AZURE_WEBAPP_PUBLISH }}
          package: './dist'
```

Combine this with **Azure Blue-Green Deployments** or **Deployment Slots** for safe rollouts.

Monitoring, Diagnostics, and Observability

Enable observability per tenant:

- Log `TenantId` in custom telemetry (App Insights)

- Build **Workbooks** to visualize tenant metrics

- Set alerts for tenant-specific SLAs or thresholds

- Monitor usage spikes, latency, or errors

App Insights Telemetry (Custom Dimensions)

```
telemetryClient.TrackEvent("OrderCreated", new Dictionary<string,
string> {
  { "TenantId", tenantId.ToString() }
});
```

Performance and Scalability

- Use **App Service Plans with Autoscaling**

- Cache frequent queries with **Azure Redis Cache**

- Offload tasks to **Azure Functions** or **Service Bus**

- Optimize DB performance with **elastic pools** or **partitioning**

Use **Front Door** or **Application Gateway** for global routing and SSL termination.

Security and Compliance

- Store secrets in **Azure Key Vault**

- Use **Managed Identity** for secure service-to-service communication

- Enforce HTTPS, CORS, and rate limits

- Conduct regular **penetration testing**

- Support **GDPR** and **data residency** requirements

Best Practices

- Design with **multi-tenancy** in mind from the start

- Use **feature flags** to enable per-tenant customization

- Secure API endpoints with **OAuth2 + RBAC**

- Automate tenant provisioning workflows

- Monitor tenant behavior to drive retention and upsell

- Separate environments (Dev/Test/Prod) using infrastructure as code

---

Summary

Azure provides a powerful, scalable, and secure foundation for building SaaS applications. Whether you're building a customer-facing product, an enterprise platform, or a B2B service, Azure services like App Service, AD B2C, SQL Database, and Logic Apps give you the tools to launch quickly and grow confidently. By architecting with multi-tenancy, automating lifecycle processes, and monitoring tenant activity, you can deliver a reliable and profitable SaaS product to customers around the world.

Key Takeaways:

- Azure is ideal for building scalable SaaS platforms with minimal overhead.

- Use B2C for customer identity and RLS or separate databases for data isolation.

- Automate provisioning, billing, and monitoring to reduce manual work.

- Apply best practices around CI/CD, observability, and DevSecOps.

- Design for scale, agility, and tenant customization from day one.

In the next section, we'll explore how to **migrate legacy applications** to Azure, modernizing your stack while preserving business continuity and minimizing risk.

Migrating Legacy Applications to Azure

Migrating legacy applications to the cloud is a strategic imperative for many organizations seeking agility, scalability, security, and cost optimization. However, moving decades-old software and infrastructure to a cloud-native environment like Azure can be complex, involving a blend of modernization, rehosting, refactoring, and rearchitecting. Azure provides a comprehensive suite of tools, services, and methodologies that enable enterprises to migrate legacy applications in a structured, low-risk, and value-driven manner.

In this section, we will explore the various strategies and phases of legacy migration to Azure. We'll cover readiness assessments, migration planning, lift-and-shift execution, modernization techniques, database migration, hybrid approaches, and best practices. Whether you're dealing with mainframe apps, legacy .NET, Java workloads, or on-premises monoliths, Azure has the tooling and guidance to ensure a successful transformation.

The Case for Migration

Legacy systems are often:

- Expensive to maintain

- Difficult to scale

- Dependent on obsolete technologies

- Challenging to secure and integrate

- Lacking real-time insights and analytics

Migrating to Azure offers:

- **Lower TCO** (Total Cost of Ownership)

- **Elastic scalability**

- **High availability**

- **Built-in compliance and security**

- **Access to modern services** (e.g., AI, containers, serverless)

Migration Strategies: The "6 R's"

Azure migration strategies are often categorized under the "6 R's" model:

1. **Rehost** – Lift-and-shift as-is using VMs or containers.

2. **Refactor** – Modify application to use cloud-native services (e.g., PaaS).

3. **Rearchitect** – Redesign to decouple monoliths into microservices.

4. **Rebuild** – Completely rewrite using modern stacks (rare and costly).

5. **Replace** – Swap with SaaS (e.g., Salesforce, Dynamics).

6. **Retire/Retain** – Decommission or keep on-prem if needed.

Most migrations begin with **rehosting**, then progressively refactor or rearchitect based on evolving business needs.

Migration Process Phases

1. **Assess**

   - Inventory existing applications and infrastructure

   - Analyze dependencies, performance, compliance needs

   - Use tools like **Azure Migrate, App Service Migration Assistant**, or **TAP**

2. **Plan**

   - Choose target Azure services and regions

   - Define landing zones (network, identity, security)

   - Determine migration order and timeline

   - Identify modernization candidates

3. **Migrate**

   - Execute rehosting, database migration, and cutover

   - Validate functionality and performance

   - Use automation tools to reduce risk

4. **Optimize**

- ○ Rightsize VMs and services

- ○ Apply autoscaling and cost governance

- ○ Monitor performance, errors, and logs

5. **Modernize**

- ○ Refactor tightly coupled services into APIs

- ○ Move from VMs to containers or serverless

- ○ Introduce CI/CD, infrastructure as code (IaC), and DevOps pipelines

---

Using Azure Migrate

Azure Migrate is the centralized migration hub for discovery, assessment, and migration.

Setup Process

1. Create Azure Migrate project from the portal.

2. Download the **Azure Migrate Appliance** to scan on-prem systems.

3. Run discovery and collect metadata (CPU, memory, disk, OS).

4. Perform assessments with cost and compatibility recommendations.

Supported Scenarios

- Windows and Linux servers

- VMware and Hyper-V

- Web apps

- Databases (SQL, Oracle, MySQL)

- Virtual desktops and VDI workloads

Rehosting Legacy Apps with Azure VM

Legacy apps tightly coupled to Windows OS or proprietary runtimes can be migrated to **Azure Virtual Machines**.

Tools

- **Azure Site Recovery (ASR)** for VM replication

- **Azure Backup** for snapshot protection

- **DSC or Ansible** for configuration

Example: Windows Server Migration

```
az vm create \
  --name LegacyAppVM \
  --resource-group LegacyApps \
  --image Win2022Datacenter \
  --size Standard_D4s_v3 \
  --admin-username azureuser \
  --generate-ssh-keys
```

Install IIS or app binaries post-migration using DSC or scripts.

Refactoring to Azure App Services

Some .NET or Java legacy apps can be moved to **Azure App Service** without full rearchitecture.

Benefits

- No server management

- Built-in load balancing and scaling

- Integrated CI/CD

- Monitoring with Application Insights

Migration Assistant

Use App Service Migration Assistant to:

- Scan IIS-hosted apps

- Package and deploy to App Service

- Analyze compatibility and dependencies

Configuration

```
az webapp create \
  --name legacywebapp \
  --plan AppServicePlan \
  --resource-group LegacyApps
```

Upload app package, set environment variables, and connect to backend database.

Modernizing the Database Layer

Move from legacy databases (SQL Server, Oracle, MySQL) to **Azure SQL**, **Cosmos DB**, or **PostgreSQL**.

Tools

- **Azure Database Migration Service (DMS)**

- **Data Migration Assistant (DMA)** for schema validation

- **BACPAC**, **Replication**, or **Backup/Restore**

Sample: SQL Server to Azure SQL Database

```
az sql db create \
  --resource-group MyRG \
  --server my-sql-server \
  --name LegacyAppDB \
  --service-objective S3
```

Use DMS to transfer data with minimal downtime.

Hybrid and Phased Migration

Some workloads must stay on-premises due to regulation or latency. Use hybrid patterns:

- **ExpressRoute or VPN** for secure connectivity

- **Azure Arc** to manage on-prem VMs and services like Azure resources

- **Azure Stack HCI** for running Azure workloads locally

- **Blob Tiering and Backup** to offload storage costs

Gradually shift pieces of the application (e.g., frontend, reporting) to the cloud before a full cutover.

Observability and Cost Management

- Use **Azure Monitor** and **Log Analytics** to track health

- Configure **alerts** and **dashboards**

- Monitor using **Application Insights** for legacy .NET apps

- Apply **Cost Management + Budgets** to control post-migration spend

Security Enhancements

Migration offers the chance to enhance security posture:

- Replace local secrets with **Azure Key Vault**

- Enable **Azure Defender for Servers**

- Apply **RBAC**, **NSGs**, and **Firewall rules**

- Use **Microsoft Defender for Cloud** to scan workloads

CI/CD and DevOps Integration

Post-migration, set up CI/CD to improve agility:

- Use **GitHub Actions** or **Azure DevOps Pipelines**

- Containerize legacy services where feasible

- Store config as code using **Bicep** or **Terraform**

- Set up **release gates**, **approvals**, and **rollback plans**

Sample Modernization Flow

1. Migrate web frontend to App Service

2. Move database to Azure SQL

3. Introduce Azure API Management for external access

4. Add Logic Apps for backend process orchestration

5. Implement telemetry and alerting

6. Refactor core business logic into containers or Functions

7. Apply cost and security governance

Best Practices

- Start with **pilot workloads** to validate approach

- Keep stakeholders informed during migration stages

- Design for **resilience and retries**

- Build rollback plans in case of failure

- Continuously optimize and modernize post-migration

- Embrace cloud-native patterns gradually (event-driven, microservices)

Summary

Migrating legacy applications to Azure allows organizations to rejuvenate aging software and infrastructure while tapping into modern cloud benefits. With a clear strategy, robust tooling, and a phased approach, even the most complex migrations can succeed. Azure enables a low-risk, high-reward transformation, unlocking agility, performance, and innovation.

Key Takeaways:

- Use Azure Migrate, App Service Migration Assistant, and DMS to simplify migration.

- Choose the right migration strategy (rehost, refactor, rearchitect).

- Begin with lift-and-shift, then incrementally modernize.

- Optimize performance, observability, and cost post-migration.

- Use hybrid tools and patterns where full migration isn't possible.

- Leverage Azure-native services for scalability and future growth.

In the next section, we will explore hybrid and multi-cloud strategies, helping you extend your applications across clouds while maintaining governance, control, and portability.

Hybrid Cloud and Multi-Cloud Strategies

As organizations evolve their IT ecosystems, many are embracing **hybrid cloud** and **multi-cloud** strategies to meet business needs around flexibility, compliance, risk management, and performance. Rather than relying solely on a single cloud vendor or on-premises infrastructure, these strategies involve using a mix of environments—including Azure, other public clouds like AWS and GCP, and private data centers—to run applications and services.

Microsoft Azure offers extensive capabilities to support hybrid and multi-cloud deployments through a combination of platform services, tools for management and monitoring, consistent security models, and integration options. Whether you're operating in highly regulated industries, managing legacy systems, or building for global availability, Azure provides the foundation to design and implement a resilient, unified hybrid/multi-cloud solution.

This section explores hybrid and multi-cloud strategies, guiding principles, architecture patterns, Azure tools like Arc and Stack, networking considerations, security implications, DevOps integration, and real-world use cases.

Definitions and Concepts

Hybrid Cloud: Combines on-premises infrastructure (data centers, private cloud) with Azure. Workloads can move between environments seamlessly, or operate in tandem.

Multi-Cloud: Utilizes services from two or more public cloud providers (e.g., Azure + AWS + GCP). Goals may include cost optimization, vendor diversification, redundancy, or proximity to specific customer regions.

Both models aim to optimize IT operations based on workload requirements rather than a one-size-fits-all solution.

Why Choose Hybrid or Multi-Cloud?

Business Drivers

- **Regulatory Compliance**: Certain data must remain on-premises due to legal or policy constraints.

- **Latency and Performance**: Local processing requirements (e.g., factory floor IoT) necessitate edge computing.

- **Vendor Resilience**: Avoiding vendor lock-in and enhancing disaster recovery options.

- **Legacy Investment**: Existing systems and data centers with long life cycles.

- **Global Reach**: Using multiple clouds to deploy closer to end-users or meet local regulations.

Azure Hybrid Services Overview

Azure provides a suite of tools and services to bridge your on-premises environment with Azure, and to manage resources across cloud providers.

Azure Service	Purpose
Azure Arc	Manage and govern hybrid/multi-cloud resources
Azure Stack HCI/Hub	Bring Azure services to on-premises environments
Azure ExpressRoute	Dedicated private connection to Azure
Azure Site Recovery	DR and failover between environments

Azure Monitor	Unified monitoring across all infrastructures
Azure Lighthouse	Manage multiple tenants at scale
Azure Policy	Enforce governance across hybrid/multi-cloud
Defender for Cloud	Unified security and compliance

Azure Arc: The Cornerstone of Hybrid/Multi-Cloud

Azure Arc extends Azure's control plane to resources outside of Azure, including:

- On-premises servers

- Kubernetes clusters

- SQL Servers

- VMs in AWS or GCP

Key Features

- Unified resource management via Azure Resource Manager

- Deploy policies, RBAC, and tags to Arc-enabled resources

- Use Azure Monitor, Defender, and Automation tools cross-cloud

- Support for GitOps-based CI/CD for Kubernetes clusters

Example: Onboarding a Server with Azure Arc

```
az connectedmachine connect \
  --resource-group ArcRG \
  --name onprem-server \
  --location eastus
```

Once connected, you can manage this server like any Azure VM using Azure Portal, CLI, or ARM templates.

Azure Stack: Bringing Azure On-Premises

Azure Stack is a family of products that brings Azure services to private and edge environments:

- **Azure Stack Hub**: Full Azure services in disconnected environments.

- **Azure Stack HCI**: Hyper-converged infrastructure for virtualized workloads.

- **Azure Stack Edge**: Appliance for edge AI, machine learning, and storage.

Use Stack for:

- Running apps in areas with limited or no connectivity

- Meeting sovereignty and data locality regulations

- Edge computing for IoT and manufacturing

Hybrid Networking

Networking is the foundation of any hybrid/multi-cloud deployment. Azure provides several services to ensure secure, performant connectivity.

Azure ExpressRoute

Establish a dedicated, private link between your data center and Azure.

- Avoids public internet

- Offers predictable performance

- Ideal for financial institutions, healthcare, and large enterprises

VPN Gateway

Site-to-site or point-to-site VPN over public internet.

- Cost-effective for smaller workloads or temporary links

- Supports high availability and active-active routing

Virtual WAN

Simplifies connectivity across branch offices, data centers, and clouds.

- Centralized network management

- Integration with third-party SD-WAN solutions

Peering and Routing

Use **VNet Peering**, **UDR**, **NVA**, and **BGP** to connect multi-cloud environments securely.

Data Synchronization and Movement

Hybrid applications often require data to flow between environments.

Azure File Sync

Synchronize on-premises Windows File Server shares with Azure Files.

- Centralized management

- Cloud-tiering reduces local storage needs

Azure Data Factory

- Supports hybrid data movement between on-premises and cloud

- Connects to over 100 data sources (SQL, SAP, Oracle, AWS S3)

Database Sync

- Use SQL Data Sync or transactional replication for hybrid SQL environments

- Enable multi-directional sync or read-only replicas

Security and Compliance

Hybrid architectures increase surface area and complexity. Azure provides a consistent security model.

- **Azure AD and AD Connect** for unified identity

- **Conditional Access** and **MFA** policies across environments

- **Azure Defender for Cloud** with support for AWS and GCP

- **Microsoft Purview** for data classification, governance, and risk management

- **Azure Key Vault and HSM** for secrets management across clouds

Use **Azure Blueprints** and **Policy** to enforce configurations organization-wide.

DevOps in a Hybrid/Multi-Cloud World

Azure DevOps and GitHub Actions can deploy across multiple environments and cloud providers.

Example: Deploy to Azure and AWS from GitHub Actions

```
jobs:
  deploy:
    steps:
      - uses: actions/checkout@v3

      # Azure Deployment
      - uses: azure/login@v1
        with:
          creds: ${{ secrets.AZURE_CREDENTIALS }}

      - run: |
          az webapp deploy ...

      # AWS Deployment
      - uses: aws-actions/configure-aws-credentials@v2
        with:
          aws-access-key-id: ${{ secrets.AWS_ACCESS_KEY }}
          aws-secret-access-key: ${{ secrets.AWS_SECRET_KEY }}

      - run: |
          aws s3 cp ./build s3://mybucket/ --recursive
```

GitOps with Azure Arc and Kubernetes

- Use Git repos as a single source of truth

- Declaratively manage AKS, GKE, EKS clusters via Arc

- Enforce configurations using Flux or ArgoCD

Use Cases

Disaster Recovery and Business Continuity

- Primary in Azure, failover to AWS or on-premises via Site Recovery or Arc

- Cross-cloud database replication

- Geo-redundant storage with paired regions

Data Residency and Sovereignty

- Store sensitive data on-prem or in a local cloud provider

- Process anonymized or non-sensitive data in Azure

- Use Azure Stack Hub for offline environments (e.g., oil rigs, military)

Performance Optimization

- Deploy frontend in GCP for Asia-Pacific

- Backend logic in Azure for secure data processing

- Use Traffic Manager or Front Door for latency-based routing

---

Best Practices

- Establish a **cloud center of excellence** (CCoE)

- Use **tagging** and **naming conventions** consistently

- Monitor everything centrally with **Azure Monitor** and **Log Analytics**

- Create a **network topology diagram** and update frequently

- Align governance policies using **Azure Policy** and **Defender**

- Test failover scenarios regularly

- Use **IaC** (Terraform, Bicep) for provisioning across clouds

- Keep your **identity and access management centralized**

Summary

Hybrid and multi-cloud strategies enable organizations to modernize at their own pace while addressing diverse operational, compliance, and technical needs. With Azure's robust ecosystem—spanning Azure Arc, Stack, networking, security, and management tools—you can confidently architect, deploy, and operate in a distributed cloud environment.

Key Takeaways:

- Hybrid and multi-cloud are complementary approaches to cloud adoption.

- Use **Azure Arc** for unified management of external and non-Azure resources.

- **Azure Stack** enables cloud capabilities on-premises or in edge environments.

- Implement strong **networking**, **security**, and **DevOps** practices across all environments.

- Treat all clouds and environments as part of a unified system with centralized policies, logging, and governance.

Next, we'll turn our attention to **cost optimization and budget management**, where we explore how to maximize ROI and efficiency across your cloud investments.

Cost Optimization and Budget Management

One of the most compelling benefits of cloud computing is its potential for cost efficiency—pay only for what you use, scale dynamically, and avoid large upfront infrastructure investments. However, without a clear understanding and control of your cloud usage, costs can quickly spiral out of control. Azure provides a comprehensive set of tools and best practices to help organizations monitor, manage, and optimize their spending while maintaining performance, availability, and business continuity.

This section explores key cost optimization principles, Azure services for budget and cost management, techniques for rightsizing resources, strategies for maximizing discounts, and real-world recommendations for establishing a culture of cost-awareness across engineering and operations teams.

Principles of Cost Optimization

Cost optimization is not a one-time activity—it requires continuous visibility, governance, and refinement across every stage of the cloud lifecycle.

Core Principles

1. **Visibility**: Understand where money is being spent, by whom, and for what.

2. **Accountability**: Assign ownership for spend to teams, projects, or departments.

3. **Efficiency**: Choose the most cost-effective services and configurations.

4. **Governance**: Define policies and enforce compliance.

5. **Automation**: Use automation to eliminate waste and reduce manual oversight.

These principles form the foundation of a successful FinOps (Financial Operations) culture that aligns engineering and finance around cloud spending goals.

Azure Cost Management and Billing

Azure Cost Management + Billing is the primary portal for managing cloud finances in Azure.

Features

- **Cost analysis dashboards**: View usage trends, anomalies, and forecasts.

- **Budgets**: Set spending limits and alerts.

- **Recommendations**: Optimize underused resources.

- **Exports**: Export raw data to Excel or Power BI.

- **Tag-based tracking**: Attribute spend to departments or environments.

Creating a Budget

1. Go to Azure Portal > Cost Management + Billing > Budgets

2. Choose subscription or resource group scope

3. Define a name, amount, and time range (monthly, quarterly)

4. Add thresholds (e.g., 80%, 100%) and email recipients for alerts

Example CLI

```
az consumption budget create \
  --amount 500 \
  --category cost \
  --name DevBudget \
  --resource-group DevTeamRG \
  --time-grain Monthly \
  --start-date 2024-01-01 \
  --end-date 2024-12-31 \
  --notifications \
    actualGreaterThan=80%:email@example.com
```

Tagging and Resource Organization

Tags allow you to assign metadata to resources for cost tracking, automation, and compliance.

Examples

```
az tag create --name Environment --value Production
az tag create --name Department --value Finance
```

Apply tags during deployment via ARM templates, Bicep, Terraform, or manually.

```
"tags": {
  "Environment": "Development",
  "Owner": "TeamAlpha",
  "CostCenter": "CC1001"
}
```

Use tags to:

*   Break down spend by team, app, or environment

- Track costs by client or tenant in multi-tenant SaaS

- Automate shutdowns or retention policies

Resource Optimization Strategies

Right-Sizing

Analyze resource utilization and resize accordingly:

- **VMs**: Use Azure Advisor to downsize underutilized VMs

- **App Services**: Move to lower-tier SKUs or use autoscaling

- **Databases**: Adjust DTU/VCores based on workload patterns

Reserved Instances (RI)

Commit to one- or three-year terms for significant discounts (up to 72%) on:

- Virtual Machines

- SQL Database compute

- App Service Environments

- Cosmos DB throughput

Best for predictable workloads with consistent usage.

```
az reservations reservation-order purchase --reserved-resource-type
VirtualMachines
```

Azure Hybrid Benefit

Reuse existing on-premises Windows Server or SQL Server licenses to reduce VM costs.

Spot VMs

Run interruptible workloads (e.g., batch jobs, CI pipelines) at a lower cost with Spot VMs.

```
az vm create \
  --name SpotVM \
```

```
--priority Spqt \
--max-price -1
```

Use with autoscaling and fault-tolerant architecture.

Automation for Cost Reduction

Auto-Shutdown and Auto-Start

Enable auto-shutdown for dev/test VMs:

```
az vm auto-shutdown --resource-group DevRG --name dev-vm --time 1800
```

Use **Azure Automation Runbooks** or **Logic Apps** to stop non-critical workloads during off-hours.

Schedule-Based Scaling

- Use **Azure Functions** or **Azure Automation** to scale resources based on time-of-day or week

- Scale in App Service Plans, VMSS, or AKS node pools

Cleanup Unused Resources

- Identify and remove unattached disks, public IPs, and orphaned NICs

- Review **Azure Advisor** regularly for cost-saving suggestions

---

Storage Cost Management

Azure storage pricing varies based on:

- Access tier (Hot, Cool, Archive)

- Redundancy (LRS, ZRS, GRS)

- Transaction count

- Data retrieval

Best Practices

- Move infrequently accessed blobs to Cool/Archive tier

- Use **Azure Blob Lifecycle Management** for automatic tiering and deletion

```json
{
  "rules": [
    {
      "enabled": true,
      "type": "Lifecycle",
      "definition": {
        "filters": {
          "blobTypes": ["blockBlob"],
          "prefixMatch": ["logs/"]
        },
        "actions": {
          "baseBlob": {
            "tierToCool": { "daysAfterModificationGreaterThan": 30
},
            "delete": { "daysAfterModificationGreaterThan": 365 }
          }
        }
      }
    }
  ]
}
```

SaaS and PaaS Cost Efficiency

PaaS services generally provide better cost-performance ratio than IaaS, with built-in scaling, patching, and availability.

Examples

- **App Services** instead of IIS on VMs

- **Azure SQL Database** instead of self-hosted SQL Server

- **Cosmos DB serverless** for infrequent queries

- **Azure Functions Premium Plan** for predictable, low-latency workloads

Use **elastic pools** to share database resources across tenants or services.

Monitoring and Alerts

Set up alerts for spending anomalies or unexpected spikes.

Example: Budget Alert

1. Go to **Cost Alerts > Create**

2. Set threshold (e.g., 120% of forecast)

3. Choose action group: email, webhook, Teams, or Logic App

Monitor Metrics with Azure Monitor

Use **metric-based alerts** to track:

- CPU/memory spikes (potential overprovisioning)

- Unused resources (e.g., idle App Services)

- Storage transaction patterns

Reporting and Forecasting

Use **Power BI** to visualize and forecast cloud spending.

- Connect directly to Cost Management exports

- Build reports by team, subscription, workload

- Model spend across regions, services, and growth trends

Use **Forecasting API** to retrieve projected costs:

```
az consumption usage forecast show --grain monthly
```

Building a FinOps Culture

A successful cost optimization strategy requires collaboration between engineering, finance, and operations teams.

Steps to Build a Cost-Aware Culture

- Share cost reports during sprint reviews or planning meetings

- Set team-based budgets and track spend against objectives

- Reward cost-saving initiatives and highlight optimizations

- Use cost KPIs (cost per tenant, per user, per transaction)

- Integrate cost planning into CI/CD and architectural decisions

---

Best Practices

- Tag resources consistently from day one

- Use resource groups to isolate environments

- Enable Azure Advisor and review monthly

- Set budgets for every subscription and resource group

- Schedule non-production resource shutdowns

- Use reservations and hybrid benefit strategically

- Visualize spend with Power BI dashboards

- Review and refactor long-lived workloads annually

Summary

Azure provides all the tools needed to manage cloud costs effectively, but real value is only achieved through continuous awareness, proactive optimization, and cross-functional collaboration. By combining cost visibility with automation, governance, and architectural best practices, organizations can unlock the full economic potential of the cloud.

Key Takeaways:

- Use **Azure Cost Management + Budgets** to track and control spending.

- Apply tags, policies, and reports to assign accountability.

- Optimize compute, storage, and database usage through right-sizing, reservations, and tiering.

- Automate cost-saving actions using Logic Apps, Functions, and Azure Automation.

- Build a FinOps culture by aligning cost control with engineering practices.

In the next chapter, we'll focus on how to **future-proof your Azure skills**, stay updated with evolving technologies, and explore learning paths, certifications, and career opportunities in the Azure ecosystem.

Chapter 8: Future-Proofing Your Azure Skills

Staying Updated with Azure Innovations

The pace of innovation in cloud computing is rapid and relentless. Microsoft Azure, as one of the leading cloud platforms, evolves daily—with new services, features, pricing tiers, security enhancements, and architectural best practices continuously being introduced. For developers, architects, and DevOps professionals working within the Azure ecosystem, keeping up with these changes is not optional—it's essential to stay relevant, effective, and competitive in a cloud-first world.

This section focuses on practical, strategic, and sustainable methods to stay updated with Azure innovations. We'll explore official resources, community-driven knowledge bases, changelogs, social channels, insider programs, sandboxing practices, and habits that successful Azure professionals adopt to remain future-ready.

The Case for Continuous Learning

Staying updated is more than skimming release notes. It means:

- **Proactively adopting** new technologies that deliver value

- **Avoiding technical debt** by not relying on deprecated tools

- **Improving security posture** by implementing latest best practices

- **Providing better solutions** to clients, users, or internal stakeholders

- **Maintaining certifications and career growth**

Because Azure evolves almost daily, even a few months of knowledge stagnation can lead to outdated practices or missing critical improvements.

Microsoft's Official Channels

Microsoft provides numerous first-party resources to help users stay informed.

Azure Updates Portal

- URL: https://azure.microsoft.com/updates

- Lists all product announcements, public previews, GA releases, and retirements

- Filter by product, region, and category

Example Use Case

Track upcoming breaking changes:

```
az provider register --namespace Microsoft.AzureActiveDirectory
# Stay aware of changes in service APIs and providers
```

Azure Blog

- URL: https://techcommunity.microsoft.com/t5/azure/ct-p/Azure

- Deep dives, case studies, feature announcements, and future roadmap insights

- Written by Microsoft product teams and field engineers

Azure Roadmap

- URL: https://azure.microsoft.com/en-us/roadmap

- Highlights upcoming features and services (planned, in preview, in development)

- Use this to anticipate integrations or changes to architectural choices

Microsoft Learn Blog and Monthly Recaps

- Monthly "What's new in Azure" recaps provide a snapshot of all changes across the ecosystem

---

Microsoft Learn and Documentation

Microsoft Learn Platform

- URL: https://learn.microsoft.com

- Thousands of free, hands-on modules

- Tracks your progress and recommends paths based on skill level

- Includes sandbox environments for testing new Azure features

Docs Updates RSS

- Documentation pages are version-controlled and updated in near real-time

- You can subscribe to page-specific changelogs via RSS feeds

Example:

To stay updated on Azure Kubernetes Service docs:

```
Subscribe to: https://learn.microsoft.com/en-us/azure/aks/whats-
new/rss.xml
```

Social Media and Community Forums

Twitter/X (Tech/Cloud Influencers)

Follow these key accounts:

- @Azure

- @MSAzureAcademy

- @MarkRussinovich (CTO of Azure)

- @MicrosoftDev

- @AzureFunctions

- @AzureArc

Use hashtags like #Azure, #MSIgnite, #AzOps, and #AzureDevOps for real-time updates.

LinkedIn

Join groups like:

- "Microsoft Azure Professionals"

- "Azure Cloud Architects"

- "CloudOps and DevOps for Azure"

Microsoft team members often announce previews and case studies here first.

Reddit

- Subreddits like `r/AZURE`, `r/CloudComputing`, and `r/devops`

- Developer-friendly, often more opinionated but full of practical insight

Stack Overflow and GitHub

- Watch repositories of SDKs and Azure CLI for commits and issues

- Great way to find out about breaking changes and early community feedback

---

Insider Programs and Early Access

Azure Insider Programs

- **Private Preview Programs**: Apply via your Microsoft account manager or Azure MVP sponsorship

- **Azure Dev/Test Labs**: Try new features in isolation

- **Azure Feature Flags (Preview APIs)**: Enable in subscription for testing under-the-hood functionality

Benefits

- Early access to innovations

- Direct feedback loop with Azure engineers

- Influence roadmap for services you depend on

Experimentation and Sandboxing

Practical experimentation is one of the best ways to learn and retain new information.

Dev/Test Subscriptions

Azure offers discounted subscriptions for learning and experimentation.

```
az account set --subscription "Visual Studio Enterprise"
# Ideal for low-risk sandbox testing
```

Free Tier Services

- Always-free services include Azure App Services, Cosmos DB, Functions, and Logic Apps

- Ideal for testing limits, performance, and feature compatibility

Deployment Slot Testing

Use App Service deployment slots or feature flags to test innovations in production-like environments before full rollout.

Azure CLI, SDKs, and APIs

Track CLI and SDK version history to understand changes:

```
az --version
az upgrade
```

Subscribe to changelogs:

- Azure CLI GitHub: https://github.com/Azure/azure-cli

- Azure SDK Releases: https://azure.github.io/azure-sdk/releases

These help you identify deprecated commands, new flags, or breaking changes in automation scripts.

Events, Conferences, and Webinars

Attend or watch recordings of:

Microsoft Ignite

- Annual global conference for IT and Dev professionals

- New service launches, architecture guidance, and expert panels

Microsoft Build

- Developer-focused announcements

- Demos of bleeding-edge features and integrations

Azure Friday

- Weekly show hosted by Scott Hanselman

- Demos of new tools and best practices

Reactor Meetups and Virtual Training Days

- Free regional sessions on specific Azure technologies

- Great for interactive Q&A and networking

Community-Led Resources

Blogs and Newsletters

- Thomas Maurer, Daniel Krzyczkowski, and other Azure MVPs maintain detailed blogs

- Subscribe to newsletters like Azure Weekly, CloudSkills.io, or The Azure Dispatch

YouTube Channels

- Microsoft Azure YouTube Channel

- John Savill's Technical Training

- Cloud Advocate demo walkthroughs

Knowledge Tracking and Habit Formation

Create a Learning Loop

1. **Discover** via blog/newsletter/event

2. **Experiment** in a sandbox or dev subscription

3. **Document** your findings or publish a blog/LinkedIn post

4. **Teach** internally or to the community

5. **Apply** to production or upcoming projects

Weekly Habits

- Read Azure Updates every Monday

- Watch a session or demo every Wednesday

- Join one community discussion every Friday

Monthly Habits

- Review subscription spend and service usage

- Update automation scripts and IaC templates with latest API versions

- Check for new preview services relevant to your project roadmap

Best Practices

- Subscribe to Azure Updates RSS and relevant service changelogs

- Use tags and naming conventions to track services in transition

- Allocate time for R&D in your sprint planning

- Maintain a personal or team Azure changelog

- Stay engaged with the Azure MVP and community ecosystem

- Use feature flags and deployment slots to adopt changes safely

- Create a backlog of "tech spikes" to experiment with new services

---

Summary

Azure is constantly evolving—and so must your skills. Staying updated is not just about checking a website now and then; it's about forming habits, leveraging community knowledge, applying what you learn, and embedding continuous education into your professional rhythm. With the right resources, proactive experimentation, and a curious mindset, you'll always be ready for what's next in the Azure ecosystem.

Key Takeaways:

- Use Microsoft's official resources and insider programs for authoritative updates

- Follow community leaders and discussions to gain practical insights

- Create sandbox environments to test features safely and regularly

- Automate tracking of CLI, SDK, and API changes

- Attend conferences and training to sharpen skills and network

- Establish learning habits and integrate them into your workflow

In the next section, we'll explore the best **community and learning resources** that support your ongoing development as an Azure practitioner, including forums, courses, certifications, and real-world project opportunities.

Community and Learning Resources

In the ever-evolving world of cloud computing, staying isolated can limit your growth. The Microsoft Azure ecosystem thrives because of its vibrant, diverse, and collaborative community. Whether you're a beginner, a seasoned professional, or someone transitioning into cloud from another domain, tapping into the Azure community and leveraging robust learning resources can accelerate your growth, increase your confidence, and help you build real-world solutions more effectively.

This section dives into the various community-driven and official resources that support your Azure learning journey. From forums and user groups to certifications, labs, blogs, and open-source contributions, we'll explore how to leverage collective knowledge, stay connected, and continuously improve your Azure skills in an engaging and meaningful way.

Why Community Matters

Being part of the Azure community allows you to:

- Get help from peers and experts

- Share your knowledge and give back

- Stay motivated and accountable

- Build a professional network

- Discover real-world use cases and implementation stories

- Gain visibility and potentially career opportunities

The Azure ecosystem is too broad for one person to master alone. Community fills in the gaps, contextualizes the documentation, and makes learning collaborative instead of solitary.

Microsoft Learn

What It Offers

- Free, modular learning paths for every Azure role (developer, admin, architect, security engineer, etc.)

- Hands-on labs with sandbox environments

- Role-based certification prep material

- Learning progress tracking with gamified achievements

Example Path

```
Learning Path: Develop for Azure Storage
- Introduction to Azure Storage
- Blob storage fundamentals
- Manage data using .NET SDK
- Practice with interactive sandbox
```

How to Maximize It

- Bookmark your current learning path

- Set weekly learning goals (e.g., 2 hours/week)

- Take notes and screenshots for reference

- Use sandboxes before applying in real projects

URL: https://learn.microsoft.com/en-us/training/

Microsoft Q&A and Tech Community

Microsoft Q&A

This is the official support and community-driven Q&A platform for Azure.

- Covers every Azure service

- Direct input from Microsoft employees

- Searchable by tags, product, and popularity

Sample question:

```
Q: How do I configure Azure Application Gateway with a Web App and
Custom Domain?
A: Detailed walkthrough provided with architecture diagram and ARM
snippet
```

Microsoft Tech Community

A broader forum that includes:

- Blog posts

- Discussions

- Event announcements

- Product feedback channels

It's a place to engage in deeper technical conversation, share ideas, and follow specific interest groups like "Azure DevOps," "Azure Security," or "Hybrid Cloud."

URL: https://techcommunity.microsoft.com/

GitHub and Open Source Repositories

Microsoft has embraced open source deeply. Azure SDKs, CLI tools, Bicep, ARM templates, and many reference architectures are open-source.

Key GitHub Repositories

- Azure CLI: https://github.com/Azure/azure-cli

- Bicep: https://github.com/Azure/bicep

- Azure SDK for .NET, JavaScript, Python, Java

- Azure Quickstart Templates: https://github.com/Azure/azure-quickstart-templates

Contribution Ideas

- Fix documentation typos or bugs

- Add new use-case examples to sample repos

- File meaningful issues or enhancement suggestions

- Engage in discussion threads to share use cases

Open-source contributions improve your understanding and give you industry visibility.

User Groups and Meetups

Join Azure-focused community groups in your region or virtually.

Where to Find Them

- https://www.meetup.com

- https://developer.microsoft.com/en-us/reactor/

- Local user group websites

Types of Events

- Hands-on labs and workshops

- Tech talks and product demos

- Certification bootcamps

- Hackathons

- Roundtable discussions

You'll meet professionals across roles—from DevOps engineers to CTOs—who face similar challenges and are often eager to share.

Blogs, Newsletters, and Podcasts

Blogs to Follow

- **Microsoft Azure Blog**: Official news and insights

- **John Savill's Blog**: Deep technical dives and certification prep

- **Scott Hanselman**: Developer-focused content with a mix of culture

- **Azure Citadel**: Hands-on labs and architecture articles

Newsletters

- **Azure Weekly**: Curated content, job posts, and news

- **Build5Nines**: Azure news with DevOps and data focus

- **The Azure Dispatch**: Cloud-native and enterprise updates

Subscribe via email or RSS to stay current.

Podcasts

- **Azure Friday**: Hosted by Scott Hanselman, with Microsoft engineers as guests

- **The Azure Podcast**: Technical discussions and use cases

- **CloudSkills.fm**: DevOps, cloud careers, and trends

- **Microsoft Cloud Show**: Broad cloud coverage including Azure, Office 365, and Power Platform

---

Certification Communities

Certifications are a structured way to benchmark skills and open new career doors.

Microsoft Certifications

Popular Azure certifications include:

- AZ-900: Azure Fundamentals

- AZ-104: Azure Administrator

- AZ-204: Azure Developer

- AZ-305: Azure Solutions Architect

- SC-300: Identity and Access Administrator

- DP-203: Data Engineering on Azure

Study Groups and Forums

- LinkedIn groups for exam takers

- Reddit's r/AzureCertification

- Discord and Slack groups dedicated to each exam

- YouTube bootcamps and guided study series

You'll find flashcards, cheat sheets, practice questions, and peer support.

Developer Communities

Stack Overflow

- Highly active Azure tags: `azure-functions`, `azure-devops`, `azure-storage`, `bicep`

- Practical, code-level discussions and solutions

Dev.to and Medium

- Developer-written tutorials with screenshots, code samples, and deployment walk-throughs

- Often cover real-world implementation patterns and postmortems

Hashnode and LinkedIn Articles

- Short posts by developers about lessons learned in production

- Insights into tool integrations, architectural decisions, and emerging best practices

Real-World Learning via Projects

One of the most effective ways to solidify Azure skills is to build or contribute to real projects.

Ideas

- Deploy a multi-region web app with Azure Front Door

- Build an IoT dashboard using Azure IoT Hub and Time Series Insights

- Containerize a legacy app with Azure Container Apps or AKS

- Build an event-driven architecture with Functions and Event Grid

Document your progress as blog posts or GitHub READMEs. Share with the community to get feedback and recognition.

Events and Hackathons

Microsoft Reactor Events

- Free technical sessions, workshops, and community meetups

- Run virtually and globally

Microsoft Learn Student Ambassadors

- University-level community led by students for students

- Offers mentorship and Microsoft-sponsored projects

Azure Dev Hack and Global Azure Bootcamp

- Community-led global events

- Solve real-world problems in teams using Azure technologies

Best Practices

- Join at least one active online community (e.g., Tech Community, Discord, Reddit)

- Attend or speak at a user group or meetup every quarter

- Subscribe to 2–3 newsletters that match your role

- Contribute to or fork one GitHub repo per month

- Use Microsoft Learn to build a structured roadmap

- Follow 5–10 Azure professionals across platforms

- Share your own findings and lessons learned—blogs, tweets, talks

Summary

You don't need to learn Azure in isolation. With its rich ecosystem of learners, practitioners, MVPs, and Microsoft insiders, Azure offers one of the most supportive tech communities in the world. Whether you're learning a new service, preparing for a certification, or solving a production challenge, the community is your greatest asset.

Key Takeaways:

- Use Microsoft Learn for structured, hands-on education

- Engage in forums, user groups, and Q&A platforms to learn from others

- Follow blogs, newsletters, and podcasts to stay in the loop

- Contribute to GitHub and Stack Overflow to grow your reputation and skills

- Build a network of peers and mentors through meetups and events

- Practice with real projects and document your journey for maximum growth

In the next section, we'll look at **career paths for Azure developers**, including specializations, role expectations, salary trends, and how to shape your long-term journey in cloud technology.

Career Paths for Azure Developers

The rapid adoption of cloud computing has redefined traditional IT and software development roles. As organizations migrate to or expand in the cloud, demand for professionals with Azure expertise has surged across industries. Whether you're a software engineer, DevOps specialist, data professional, or aspiring cloud architect, there is a broad and growing spectrum of career paths available for Azure developers. Each path is uniquely shaped by the blend of your interests, domain knowledge, and level of cloud proficiency.

This section explores the main career paths for Azure developers, breaking down responsibilities, required skills, certifications, tooling, salary trends, advancement strategies, and day-to-day realities. It will help you align your Azure learning journey with meaningful professional outcomes—whether you're just starting out or planning your next big move.

The Azure Developer Career Landscape

Azure developers aren't limited to a single role. The ecosystem is expansive and evolving, creating numerous specialization opportunities. Common career paths include:

- Azure Application Developer

- Azure DevOps Engineer

- Azure Solutions Architect

- Azure Data Engineer

- Azure AI/ML Engineer

- Site Reliability Engineer (SRE)

- Cloud Security Engineer

- Cloud-native .NET or Java Developer

- Full-Stack Cloud Developer

These roles can exist within startups, enterprises, consultancies, government bodies, or as part of managed service providers (MSPs).

---

1. Azure Application Developer

Overview

These developers build, deploy, and maintain cloud-native or cloud-enhanced applications using Azure PaaS services such as App Services, Functions, Storage, and Cosmos DB.

Skills and Tools

- Languages: C#, .NET, JavaScript/TypeScript, Python

- Azure App Services, Azure Functions, Logic Apps

- Azure SDKs, Azure CLI, ARM/Bicep templates

- Application Insights, Azure Key Vault

- CI/CD with GitHub Actions or Azure DevOps

- REST API integration and OAuth2

Certification

- AZ-204: Developing Solutions for Microsoft Azure

Career Progression

- Senior Developer → Technical Lead → Solutions Architect

---

2. Azure DevOps Engineer

Overview

Combines development and operations expertise to streamline software delivery and infrastructure automation using Azure-native DevOps tools.

Skills and Tools

- Azure DevOps, GitHub Actions, Terraform/Bicep

- Azure Pipelines, Repos, Artifacts, Boards

- Docker, Kubernetes (AKS), Helm

- CI/CD pipeline creation, release management

- Monitoring and alerting with Azure Monitor

Certification

- AZ-400: Designing and Implementing Microsoft DevOps Solutions

Career Progression

- DevOps Engineer → Platform Engineer → DevOps Architect

---

3. Azure Solutions Architect

Overview

Responsible for designing scalable, secure, and cost-efficient Azure solutions across services and teams.

Skills and Tools

- Broad knowledge of Azure services (compute, storage, networking, identity)

- Architectural patterns (microservices, serverless, hybrid cloud)

- Security, compliance, and governance best practices

- Cost estimation and optimization

- Diagrams and documentation with tools like Draw.io, Lucidchart

Certification

- AZ-305: Designing Microsoft Azure Infrastructure Solutions

Career Progression

- Architect → Enterprise Architect or Cloud Strategy Lead

---

4. Azure Data Engineer

Overview

Designs and implements secure, scalable data pipelines and analytics solutions using Azure data services.

Skills and Tools

- Azure Data Factory, Synapse Analytics, Azure SQL, Cosmos DB

- Azure Storage, Delta Lake, Data Lake Gen2

- Data modeling, ETL, batch and real-time data flows

- Integration with Power BI and ML pipelines

Certification

- DP-203: Data Engineering on Microsoft Azure

Career Progression

- Data Engineer → Data Architect → Chief Data Officer

---

5. Azure AI and ML Engineer

Overview

Builds intelligent applications and machine learning workflows using Azure's AI and ML toolkits.

Skills and Tools

- Azure Cognitive Services, OpenAI, and Azure ML Studio

- Python, R, and popular ML libraries (Scikit-learn, PyTorch, TensorFlow)

- Responsible AI practices, explainability, fairness

- Data labeling, training pipelines, model deployment

Certification

- AI-102: Designing and Implementing an Azure AI Solution

Career Progression

- ML Engineer → Data Scientist → AI Lead

---

6. Site Reliability Engineer (SRE) or Cloud Operations Engineer

Overview

Ensures systems are highly available, performant, and resilient at scale using automation and observability.

Skills and Tools

- Azure Monitor, Log Analytics, Application Insights

- Infrastructure as Code (IaC) and automation scripts

- Load testing, chaos engineering, autoscaling

- Incident response, SLAs, and service health monitoring

Certification

- AZ-104 (Administrator), AZ-400 (DevOps), SC-200 (Security)

Career Progression

- SRE → Reliability Architect → Engineering Manager

7. Cloud Security Engineer

Overview

Secures Azure workloads through configuration management, threat detection, access control, and compliance enforcement.

Skills and Tools

- Azure Security Center, Defender for Cloud, Key Vault

- Azure Policy, Blueprints, RBAC, Conditional Access

- SIEM integration with Microsoft Sentinel

- Threat modeling and identity governance

Certification

- SC-200: Microsoft Security Operations Analyst

- SC-300: Identity and Access Administrator

- AZ-500: Azure Security Engineer Associate

Career Progression

- Security Analyst → Security Architect → CISO

Cross-Cutting Skills

Regardless of specialization, the following skills are valuable across Azure developer roles:

- **Version Control (Git/GitHub)**

- **RESTful API design and consumption**

- **Containerization (Docker, Container Apps, AKS)**

- **Scripting (PowerShell, Bash)**

- **Infrastructure as Code (ARM, Bicep, Terraform)**

- **Cloud cost management and optimization**

- **Monitoring and incident response**

- **Soft skills: communication, collaboration, documentation**

Industry Demand and Salary Trends

Azure roles are in high demand globally. Salaries vary by location, seniority, and company size.

Role	Average Salary (USD/year)
Azure Developer	$90,000 – $120,000
Azure DevOps Engineer	$110,000 – $140,000
Azure Solutions Architect	$130,000 – $160,000
Azure Data Engineer	$100,000 – $135,000
Azure AI Engineer	$105,000 – $145,000
Azure Security Engineer	$110,000 – $150,000

Data from industry reports and global job portals like Glassdoor, Indeed, and Payscale.

Building Your Career Roadmap

1. Identify Interests

Are you more passionate about data, operations, security, or development? Your interest should guide your specialization.

2. Map Skills to Roles

Use role guides from Microsoft Learn and certification paths to understand skill expectations.

3. Gain Experience

- Start with labs, then real-world projects

- Contribute to open source or community demos

- Intern, freelance, or shadow existing professionals

4. Earn Certifications

Validate your skills and stand out to employers. Many companies reimburse exam fees.

5. Build Your Personal Brand

- Write blogs or tutorials on what you've learned

- Share code on GitHub

- Speak at local meetups or virtual events

6. Explore Cross-Functional Roles

Move laterally into product, management, architecture, or research after gaining domain depth.

Best Practices

- Align certifications with your career goals, not trends

- Build a GitHub portfolio demonstrating relevant Azure projects

- Network through Azure community groups and LinkedIn

- Stay updated with Azure changes and roadmap

- Follow industry thought leaders and open-source maintainers

- Document every project you work on (architecture, challenges, results)

- Learn budgeting, costing, and compliance considerations for enterprise roles

---

Summary

Azure opens up a universe of career possibilities, each with its own exciting trajectory and learning curve. Whether you're solving data problems, automating deployments, or securing global-scale applications, your skills as an Azure developer will remain in high demand. Choose a path that aligns with your interests, deepen your expertise, and evolve with the platform as it grows.

Key Takeaways:

- Azure offers multiple career paths, from developer and architect to AI, DevOps, and security roles

- Each role demands a mix of core cloud skills and specialized knowledge

- Certifications, hands-on projects, and community engagement accelerate career growth

- Salaries are competitive, with strong opportunities in every sector

- Build a roadmap and revisit it regularly as your interests and the industry evolve

In the next section, we'll cover the **certification roadmap** in more detail, helping you understand which Azure certifications to pursue, how to prepare for them, and how they map to real-world career goals.

Certification Roadmap

As cloud computing continues to shape the future of technology, validating your Azure expertise through certifications has become a strategic move for professionals looking to advance their careers. Microsoft Azure certifications are globally recognized, role-based, and tailored to a wide range of skill levels—from absolute beginners to seasoned cloud architects and specialists. Whether you're breaking into tech, shifting roles, or aiming for leadership, Azure certifications offer a structured and measurable path to career progression.

This section provides a comprehensive roadmap of Azure certifications. We'll explore their structure, prerequisites, preparation strategies, exam formats, renewal processes, and how to align them with your career goals. Additionally, we'll cover how certifications fit into your long-term growth plan and how to build credibility beyond exams.

Why Azure Certifications Matter

Certifications provide:

- **Credibility**: Validate your skills to employers and clients

- **Confidence**: Reinforce your understanding of key concepts

- **Structure**: Organize your learning in a goal-oriented path

- **Opportunities**: Boost your chances in hiring pipelines

- **Community Recognition**: Gain access to exclusive Microsoft groups, events, and networks

Employers often list certifications as desirable or required in job postings, and many use them to assess technical capability, especially in the absence of professional experience.

Azure Certification Structure

Microsoft certifications are role-based and grouped into three levels:

1. **Fundamentals** – Entry-level, no experience required

2. **Associate** – Intermediate skills and practical knowledge

3. **Expert** – Advanced, typically with 2–5+ years of experience

Additionally, there are **Specialty Certifications** that target advanced niche areas like security, IoT, AI, and SAP.

Fundamentals Certifications

These are ideal for beginners or those looking to validate their foundational understanding of Azure and related technologies.

AZ-900: Microsoft Azure Fundamentals

- **Target Audience**: Beginners, students, non-technical professionals

- **Topics**: Core Azure services, pricing, SLAs, governance, security

- **Format**: Multiple-choice, drag-and-drop, scenario-based questions

- **Preparation**: Microsoft Learn, Whizlabs, John Savill YouTube series

Others

- **AI-900**: Azure AI Fundamentals

- **DP-900**: Azure Data Fundamentals

- **SC-900**: Security, Compliance, and Identity Fundamentals

These certifications are optional prerequisites for associate-level paths.

Associate Certifications

Designed for professionals who want to specialize in development, administration, data, or DevOps.

AZ-204: Developing Solutions for Microsoft Azure

- **Focus**: Building, testing, deploying apps with App Services, Functions, Cosmos DB, and APIs

- **Ideal For**: Azure developers and software engineers

- **Skills Tested**: Compute, storage, security, integrations, monitoring

AZ-104: Microsoft Azure Administrator

- **Focus**: Managing Azure resources, identity, governance, networking, and backups

- **Ideal For**: System admins, support engineers

- **Skills Tested**: Azure Portal, PowerShell, CLI, ARM templates

DP-203: Data Engineering on Microsoft Azure

- **Focus**: Data ingestion, storage, transformation, and serving

- **Ideal For**: Data engineers, analytics professionals

- **Skills Tested**: Azure Data Factory, Synapse, Cosmos DB, SQL pools

SC-300: Identity and Access Administrator

- **Focus**: Implementing identity solutions with Azure AD

- **Skills Tested**: Conditional Access, B2B/B2C, MFA, RBAC, PIM

Expert Certifications

For professionals with deep experience in planning, designing, and leading Azure solutions.

AZ-305: Designing Microsoft Azure Infrastructure Solutions

- **Prerequisite**: AZ-104 is recommended (not mandatory)

- **Focus**: Designing compute, networking, storage, identity, and governance architectures

- **Ideal For**: Solution architects

- **Exam Format**: Case studies, multiple-choice, drag-and-drop

AZ-400: Designing and Implementing Microsoft DevOps Solutions

- **Prerequisite**: Strong knowledge of Azure DevOps, CI/CD, infra automation

- **Ideal For**: DevOps engineers, SREs

- **Topics**: Continuous integration, testing, delivery, monitoring, feedback loops

---

Specialty Certifications

Focused certifications for niche, high-demand areas:

Certification	Area	Example Roles
SC-200	Security Operations Analyst	SOC Analyst, Security Engineer
SC-100	Cybersecurity Architect Expert	CISO, Security Architect
AI-102	Azure AI Engineer Associate	AI Developer, ML Engineer
MB-500	Dynamics 365 Finance & Ops Developer	ERP Developer, Solution Consultant

| AZ-120 | SAP on Azure | SAP Basis Consultant, SAP Architect |
| AZ-220 | Azure IoT Developer | Embedded Systems Dev, IoT Architect |

Certification Renewal and Expiry

Since 2021, Microsoft certifications no longer expire after two years. Instead:

- Renew annually by passing a **free online renewal assessment**

- No proctor or exam fee required

- Receive reminders 6 months before expiry

Keep your certifications current and aligned with Azure updates.

Study and Preparation Strategy

1. **Choose Your Role and Goal**

   Identify which certification aligns with your short-term and long-term career goals.

2. **Use Microsoft Learn Paths**

   Follow structured learning paths with hands-on modules and sandbox labs.

3. **Take Practice Exams**

   Providers like MeasureUp, Whizlabs, and ExamTopics offer realistic mock exams.

4. **Use Flashcards and Cheatsheets**

   Review terminology, service limits, and architectural scenarios.

5. **Join a Study Group**

   Learn with peers on Discord, Reddit, or LinkedIn. Share challenges and insights.

6. **Watch Video Courses**

   Platforms like Pluralsight, LinkedIn Learning, A Cloud Guru, and Udemy offer in-depth walkthroughs.

7. **Create a Personal Lab Environment**

   Use the Azure free tier or Visual Studio benefits to build real apps and services.

Sample Certification Paths

Developer-Focused

1. AZ-900 → AZ-204 → AZ-400 → AZ-305 (optional)

2. Add AI-102 or SC-300 for specialization

DevOps/Infra-Focused

1. AZ-900 → AZ-104 → AZ-400 → SC-100 (optional)

2. Add SC-200 or AZ-500 for security depth

Data and AI-Focused

1. DP-900 → DP-203 → AI-102 → Expert AI cert (when released)

Certification Benefits

- Access to Microsoft Certified Community

- Digital badges for LinkedIn and portfolios

- Priority at Microsoft events and webinars

- Opportunities for MVP nominations

- Confidence in client-facing roles or freelance gigs

Building a Certification Timeline

- **Month 1**: Fundamentals (AZ-900, DP-900, etc.)

- **Month 2–3**: Associate-level exam prep and labs

- **Month 4–5**: Practice exams, study groups, real-world scenarios

- **Month 6+**: Schedule and take exam, review errors post-exam

Adjust based on available time, prior experience, and exam readiness.

Best Practices

- Read the official **skills outline** before preparing

- Use real-world use cases to reinforce abstract concepts

- Don't memorize—understand how and when to apply services

- Pair certifications with **portfolio projects** for maximum impact

- Share your learning journey to inspire others

- Refresh knowledge before attempting renewal assessments

- Schedule the exam early to stay committed

Summary

Microsoft Azure certifications offer a powerful and credible way to validate your skills, advance your career, and stay competitive in a cloud-first world. Whether you're taking your first steps into cloud computing or aiming to specialize in high-impact areas like AI, DevOps, or security, there's a certification path tailored to your goals. What matters most is consistency, practical learning, and a growth mindset.

Key Takeaways:

- Azure certifications are structured by role and level: Fundamentals → Associate → Expert → Specialty

- Start with AZ-900 and branch into development, operations, data, or security

- Use Microsoft Learn, practice exams, and community groups to prepare

- Renew certifications annually through free online assessments

- Align your certification journey with real projects and long-term goals

In the next chapter, we'll explore the **Appendices**, including glossaries, additional resources, project templates, API reference guides, and answers to frequently asked questions to support your continued Azure development journey.

Chapter 9: Appendices

Glossary of Terms

Understanding Azure and cloud computing requires familiarity with a wide range of terms and acronyms. This glossary provides definitions and context for essential terms used throughout this book and within the broader Azure ecosystem. The goal is to equip you with a foundational vocabulary that enhances comprehension and communication as you work with Azure services and teams.

A

Azure Active Directory (Azure AD)
A cloud-based identity and access management service used for managing users, groups, and access to resources. Supports SSO, MFA, B2B, and B2C scenarios.

Azure Arc
A service that allows you to manage non-Azure resources (on-premises or other clouds) through the Azure control plane.

Azure App Service
A PaaS offering that allows developers to host web apps, REST APIs, and mobile backends in a fully managed environment.

Availability Set
A logical grouping of VMs that ensures redundancy by distributing them across multiple fault and update domains.

Availability Zone
Physically separate zones within an Azure region that offer high availability and fault tolerance for your applications.

B

Bicep
A domain-specific language (DSL) for deploying Azure resources declaratively. It simplifies ARM templates.

Blob Storage
A service for storing large amounts of unstructured data, such as text or binary data, typically used for images, videos, and backups.

Burstable VM (B-series)
VMs designed for workloads that do not require consistent CPU performance but occasionally burst to higher levels.

C

CI/CD (Continuous Integration/Continuous Deployment)
A development practice that automates the integration and deployment of code changes to improve development speed and reliability.

Cloud Shell
An interactive browser-accessible shell for managing Azure resources using CLI or PowerShell with pre-installed tools.

Cosmos DB
A globally distributed NoSQL database service with support for multiple APIs, low-latency, and horizontal scaling.

Content Delivery Network (CDN)
A globally distributed network of servers that deliver web content based on user geographic location, speeding up access to static files.

Container Instance (ACI)
A service to run containers in Azure without managing VMs or orchestrators.

D

Data Factory
Azure's ETL and data integration service that enables the creation of data-driven workflows.

Data Lake
A scalable repository for big data analytics workloads, often used with structured and unstructured data.

Databricks
An Apache Spark-based analytics platform optimized for Azure that supports data science, engineering, and machine learning.

Defender for Cloud
A unified security management system that provides advanced threat protection across hybrid cloud workloads.

DevOps
A cultural and technical movement focused on unifying development and operations for continuous delivery and high software quality.

E

Elastic Pool
A cost-effective way to manage and scale multiple Azure SQL databases with shared resources.

Event Grid
An event routing service that enables reactive programming by delivering events from sources to handlers.

Event Hub
A big data streaming platform and event ingestion service capable of processing millions of events per second.

ExpressRoute
A dedicated, private network connection between an on-premises network and Microsoft Azure.

F

Failover
A backup operational mode in which functions of a system are assumed by secondary systems when the primary system becomes unavailable.

Function App
The resource container for one or more Azure Functions, which are small, serverless units of logic triggered by events.

G

Geo-Replication
The process of copying and storing data across geographically diverse regions to improve availability and disaster recovery.

GitHub Actions
An automation tool for CI/CD pipelines directly integrated into GitHub.

H

Hybrid Cloud
A computing environment that combines public cloud and private infrastructure, allowing data and apps to be shared between them.

High Availability (HA)
A design approach ensuring that services remain available and operational during failures or maintenance.

I

Infrastructure as Code (IaC)
The process of managing and provisioning infrastructure using code instead of manual processes.

Ingress
The process of data entering a cloud service or system.

Instance Metadata Service (IMDS)
A REST endpoint that provides information about running VMs and other resources.

J

JSON (JavaScript Object Notation)
A lightweight data-interchange format used in Azure for defining resource templates and configuring services.

K

Key Vault
A service for storing and managing cryptographic keys, secrets, and certificates securely.

Kubernetes (AKS)
An open-source system for automating deployment, scaling, and management of containerized applications. Azure Kubernetes Service (AKS) is Azure's managed offering.

L

Latency
The time delay experienced in a system, often a concern in networking and data transfer.

Load Balancer
A networking solution that distributes incoming traffic across multiple instances to improve responsiveness and availability.

Logic Apps
A visual designer-based integration platform for automating workflows across cloud and on-prem services.

M

Managed Identity
An Azure identity used by services to authenticate to other Azure services securely without storing credentials.

Metrics
Quantitative data collected by Azure Monitor to evaluate the performance and health of applications and resources.

Monitoring
Continuous observation of system operations using tools like Azure Monitor and Application Insights.

N

Network Security Group (NSG)
A virtual firewall that controls inbound and outbound traffic to network interfaces, VMs, and subnets.

NoSQL
A category of databases that store data in non-tabular formats. Cosmos DB supports NoSQL document and key-value stores.

O

OAuth2
An open standard protocol used for authorization, enabling access delegation between services.

Outbound Traffic
Network traffic leaving an Azure resource to another service or network.

P

PaaS (Platform as a Service)
A cloud computing model that provides a platform allowing customers to develop, run, and manage applications.

Private Endpoint
A network interface that connects privately to a service, enabling private and secure communication.

Provisioning
The process of creating and configuring cloud resources based on specifications.

Q

Query Performance Insight
A feature in Azure SQL that helps diagnose and troubleshoot performance issues using queries, metrics, and recommendations.

R

RBAC (Role-Based Access Control)
A method of regulating access to resources based on user roles.

Replication
The process of synchronizing data between locations for durability and high availability.

Resource Group
A container for managing related Azure resources.

S

Scaling (Horizontal/Vertical)
The process of increasing capacity by adding more instances (horizontal) or upgrading existing resources (vertical).

Service Bus
An enterprise message broker that enables asynchronous communication between services.

Service Principal
An identity used by applications or automated tools to access Azure resources securely.

SKU (Stock Keeping Unit)
A specific configuration of an Azure resource that defines performance and pricing tier.

T

Terraform
An open-source IaC tool by HashiCorp that enables multi-cloud infrastructure provisioning, supported on Azure.

Throughput
The amount of work a system can perform in a given time, often measured in transactions per second (TPS).

U

Update Domain
A group of VMs that can be updated or rebooted at the same time. Helps prevent downtime during updates.

User-Assigned Managed Identity
A standalone managed identity created and assigned to multiple Azure resources.

V

Virtual Machine (VM)
An emulation of a physical computer running in Azure that includes CPU, memory, storage, and networking.

Virtual Network (VNet)
A logically isolated network in Azure that allows Azure resources to securely communicate.

VPN Gateway
A secure connection between on-premises networks and Azure over a public network.

W

Web App
A type of App Service designed for hosting websites and web APIs using various programming languages.

Workspace
In Azure Monitor and Log Analytics, a workspace defines the scope for data collection, queries, and alerts.

X

XML (eXtensible Markup Language)
A markup language used for data representation. Common in legacy systems and integrations.

Y

YAML (YAML Ain't Markup Language)
A human-readable data serialization format often used in configuration files, including Azure DevOps pipelines and Kubernetes manifests.

Z

Zone Redundancy
The capability of a service or resource to remain available even if one availability zone fails.

Zero Trust
A security principle that assumes no device, user, or system is trusted by default, requiring constant verification and least-privilege access.

This glossary is intended to serve as a living reference. As Azure services and terminology evolve, consider bookmarking the official Azure Glossary on the Microsoft Docs site and staying active in forums and communities to learn emerging terms in context.

In the next section, we'll provide a curated list of **resources for further learning**, including books, courses, blogs, and expert channels that can support your continued growth on your Azure development journey.

Resources for Further Learning

The journey of mastering Azure doesn't end with reading a book or earning a certification—continuous learning is vital. Azure evolves rapidly, with new features, updates, and best practices emerging daily. To keep up with this pace and remain effective in your role, it's important to establish a reliable system of continuous education. This section offers a curated and comprehensive list of learning resources categorized by type, use case, and professional goal. Whether you're looking for in-depth technical documentation, real-world coding labs, community insights, or expert-level courses, this guide will help you navigate the rich ecosystem of Azure educational materials.

Microsoft Learn

URL: https://learn.microsoft.com

Microsoft Learn is the official learning platform provided by Microsoft. It offers hundreds of guided modules, sandbox environments, learning paths, and role-based learning content.

Key Features:

- Hands-on exercises with temporary Azure subscriptions

- Role-specific learning paths (developer, architect, administrator, security engineer, etc.)

- Certification preparation content

- Progress tracking and achievements

- Integrated with GitHub for some labs

Recommended Paths:

- *Azure Fundamentals*: Great for beginners

- *Develop Azure compute solutions*: Focuses on App Services, Functions, and AKS

- *Implement CI/CD pipelines with Azure DevOps*: Ideal for DevOps engineers

- *Secure applications and services*: Relevant for developers and architects

Books and eBooks

While Azure documentation is excellent for staying current, books are valuable for structured, end-to-end understanding of topics.

Notable Titles:

- **Exam Ref AZ-204 Developing Solutions for Microsoft Azure**
  Authoritative guide for developers targeting the AZ-204 certification.

- **Microsoft Azure Architecture Best Practices**
  Comprehensive overview of designing scalable, secure, and resilient systems.

- **Azure for Architects: Design, Deploy, and Manage Cloud Solutions**
  Ideal for intermediate to expert professionals aiming for the AZ-305 exam or solutions architect roles.

- **Cloud Design Patterns**
  Covers architecture patterns in cloud-native design, available via Microsoft Press.

- **The Developer's Guide to Azure** (free eBook from Microsoft)
  Practical guide for application developers exploring Azure platforms and services.

Most of these books are available on Amazon, Microsoft Press, O'Reilly, or Packt Publishing.

Online Learning Platforms

If you prefer video-based learning, these platforms offer structured courses, projects, and certification prep.

Pluralsight

- Microsoft-partnered courses for AZ-900, AZ-104, AZ-204, and others

- Hands-on labs and skill assessments

- Courses by expert instructors like Tim Warner and Orin Thomas

A Cloud Guru / Linux Academy

- Excellent for DevOps, containers, and multi-cloud learning

- Scenario-based labs and real exam simulations

LinkedIn Learning

- Courses designed for developers, administrators, and business leaders

- Topics range from Azure DevOps to infrastructure and AI

- Integrated with LinkedIn profiles for certification sharing

Udemy

- Affordable courses covering every Azure certification and service

- Notable instructors: Scott Duffy, Alan Rodrigues, Nick Colyer

- Check reviews and update dates before purchasing

YouTube Channels and Video Series

Visual learners benefit greatly from YouTube tutorials, walkthroughs, and whiteboard sessions.

Azure Friday

- Hosted by Scott Hanselman

- Weekly deep dives into new and existing Azure services

- Interviews with Microsoft product teams

John Savill's Technical Training

- AZ-900 to AZ-305 prep videos

- Architecture series and real-world solutions

- Whiteboard and live-lab teaching style

Microsoft Developer Channel

- Tutorials, demos, and event keynotes

- Content on .NET, Azure Functions, AI, and IoT

GitHub Learning Labs (with Azure focus)

- URL: https://lab.github.com

- Interactive learning via pull requests, issues, and code contributions

Practice Labs and Sandboxes

Hands-on practice is critical for real-world readiness. Several platforms provide practice environments where you can experiment freely.

Azure Sandbox (via Microsoft Learn)

- Launches a temporary subscription for module-based exercises
- No credit card required
- Resets after each module or lab

Whizlabs & ExamPro

- Offer practice exams and labs specifically aligned with Azure certifications
- Ideal for reinforcement before taking exams

Katacoda (now part of O'Reilly)

- Interactive browser-based labs on Azure, Kubernetes, and DevOps topics

Cloud Academy

- Learning paths with real-world projects and cloud challenges
- Tracks skill progression over time

GitHub Repositories and Samples

GitHub is an invaluable resource for finding working examples, templates, and community projects.

Official Microsoft Repositories

- https://github.com/Azure/azure-quickstart-templates: Hundreds of ARM/Bicep templates for rapid provisioning
- https://github.com/Azure-Samples: Samples for SDKs, Functions, App Services, Cosmos DB, and more

- https://github.com/Azure/azure-sdk-for-js: Azure SDKs for JavaScript developers

Community Projects

- Search for "azure boilerplate," "bicep modules," or "aks workshop"

- Join GitHub Discussions for usage patterns and real feedback

Blogs and Newsletters

Azure Blog

- Official Microsoft source for product updates and roadmap

- Includes monthly "What's New" recaps

- URL: https://azure.microsoft.com/en-us/blog

Azure Weekly

- Curated list of news, tutorials, tools, and community updates

- URL: https://azureweekly.info

Build5Nines

- Technical deep dives and certification updates

- Maintained by Microsoft MVPs

Thomas Maurer, Sam Cogan, and Sarah Lean

- Blogs covering Azure automation, infrastructure, and real-world architecture tips

The Azure Dispatch

- Newsletter focused on cloud-native patterns and Azure microservices

Events, Conferences, and Recordings

Live events provide insights into what's next and access to Microsoft engineers and community leaders.

Microsoft Ignite

- Annual event with product announcements and roadmap

- Free and virtual in recent years

- Sessions available on-demand

Microsoft Build

- Developer-focused sessions covering .NET, AI, DevOps, APIs, and web

Global Azure Bootcamp

- Community-organized, free events around the world

- Hands-on labs and certifications prep

Microsoft Reactor

- Regular free events and workshops across Azure, Power Platform, and more

- URL: https://developer.microsoft.com/reactor

Discussion Forums and Communities

Microsoft Q&A

- Official forum for all Azure products

- Responses often provided by Microsoft engineers

Stack Overflow

- Active tags like `azure`, `azure-functions`, `azure-devops`, `bicep`

- Excellent for debugging and edge cases

Reddit

- Subreddits: `r/AZURE`, `r/AzureCertification`, `r/devops`

- Peer support and real-world discussions

Discord / Slack Communities

- Join Azure Study Groups or DevOps-focused servers

- Engage in real-time Q&A, study sessions, and mentoring

Career and Certification Trackers

- **CloudSkills.io Tracker**: Tracks Azure certifications, modules completed, and skills

- **Microsoft Learn Profile**: Auto-updates with progress and badges

- **Notion / Obsidian Templates**: Use personal knowledge management to track study notes and learning plans

---

Best Practices

- Mix formats: combine documentation, video, labs, and discussions

- Schedule a weekly "cloud hour" for consistent learning

- Bookmark key URLs and use RSS or newsletters to stay updated

- Follow product teams and MVPs on social media for timely insights

- Set quarterly learning goals (e.g., one certification, one project)

Summary

Your Azure learning journey doesn't end—it evolves with the platform. With the right mix of resources, community involvement, and hands-on experimentation, you can continually grow your skills and adapt to any new challenge the cloud brings. The curated resources listed here are meant to support every stage of your journey, from beginner to architect, from certification to production.

Key Takeaways:

- Microsoft Learn and GitHub are your foundational resources

- Use labs and sandboxes for experiential learning

- Engage with the community through blogs, newsletters, and forums

- Combine structured courses with real-world projects

- Attend events and workshops to stay ahead of trends

- Build a personalized learning plan and review it regularly

Next, we'll explore **sample projects and code snippets** that consolidate many of the core concepts covered throughout this book, helping you put theory into practice and build a portfolio that showcases your Azure expertise.

Sample Projects and Code Snippets

Learning Azure theoretically is important, but true mastery comes from applying that knowledge in real-world projects. Whether you're preparing for a job interview, aiming to earn a certification, or building a portfolio to showcase your cloud skills, implementing practical projects is essential. This section provides a collection of sample projects and code snippets, ranging from beginner to advanced, to help reinforce the concepts covered in this book.

Each project emphasizes different aspects of the Azure platform—compute, storage, networking, identity, automation, and DevOps—and is designed to help you get hands-on experience with the tools, services, and practices professionals use in the field.

Project 1: Deploy a Serverless API with Azure Functions and Cosmos DB

Overview

This project demonstrates how to create a lightweight, scalable API using Azure Functions and connect it to a NoSQL Cosmos DB instance.

Services Used

- Azure Functions

- Azure Cosmos DB

- Azure Portal

- Azure CLI

Steps

1. Create a resource group:

```
az group create --name ServerlessApiRG --location eastus
```

2. Create a Cosmos DB account:

```
az cosmosdb create --name ServerlessApiDB --resource-group
ServerlessApiRG --kind MongoDB
```

3. Create a new Function App:

```
az functionapp create \
  --resource-group ServerlessApiRG \
  --consumption-plan-location eastus \
  --runtime node \
  --functions-version 4 \
  --name myServerlessApi \
  --storage-account mystorageaccountapi
```

4. Implement function logic in JavaScript or Python to read/write to Cosmos DB.

5. Use Postman or curl to test HTTP triggers.

Project 2: Build a Scalable Web App with Azure App Service and SQL Database

Overview

Deploy a sample full-stack web application using Azure App Service for hosting and Azure SQL Database for persistence.

Services Used

- App Service (Web App)

- Azure SQL Database

- Azure DevOps (optional for CI/CD)

Key Code Snippet

```
az webapp up --name mywebappdemo --runtime "DOTNET|6.0" --resource-
group MyRG
```

Backend Sample (C#)

```csharp
public IActionResult GetProducts()
{
    using (SqlConnection conn = new
SqlConnection(_config.GetConnectionString("Default")))
    {
        conn.Open();
        SqlCommand cmd = new SqlCommand("SELECT * FROM Products",
conn);
        SqlDataReader reader = cmd.ExecuteReader();
        // Return product list as JSON
    }
}
```

Project 3: Automated Deployment with GitHub Actions

Overview

Set up a GitHub Actions pipeline that builds and deploys a .NET or Node.js app to Azure Web App automatically upon code push.

Workflow File: `.github/workflows/deploy.yml`

```yaml
name: Deploy to Azure

on:
  push:
    branches:
      - main

jobs:
```

```
build-and-deploy:
  runs-on: ubuntu-latest
  steps:
    - name: Checkout code
      uses: actions/checkout@v2

    - name: Login to Azure
      uses: azure/login@v1
      with:
        creds: ${{ secrets.AZURE_CREDENTIALS }}

    - name: Deploy web app
      uses: azure/webapps-deploy@v2
      with:
        app-name: 'mywebapp'
        package: '.'
```

Project 4: Event-Driven Architecture with Event Grid and Logic Apps

Overview

This solution triggers a workflow whenever a new blob is uploaded to Azure Blob Storage, demonstrating integration via Event Grid.

Services Used

- Azure Blob Storage

- Azure Event Grid

- Azure Logic Apps

Key Steps

1. Create a storage account and container.

2. Enable Event Grid on the storage account.

3. Create a Logic App with a trigger for `BlobCreated` events.

4. Add actions such as sending email, inserting data into SQL DB, or calling a webhook.

Project 5: Infrastructure as Code with Bicep

Overview

Provision a complete environment using Bicep templates for VM, NSG, VNet, and storage.

Sample Bicep Template

```
resource vnet 'Microsoft.Network/virtualNetworks@2021-05-01' = {
  name: 'myVnet'
  location: resourceGroup().location
  properties: {
    addressSpace: {
      addressPrefixes: [
        '10.0.0.0/16'
      ]
    }
  }
}
```

Deployment

```
az deployment group create \
  --resource-group MyRG \
  --template-file main.bicep
```

Project 6: Monitor Application Performance with Application Insights

Overview

Add Application Insights to a .NET web app and analyze metrics and logs.

Configuration (appsettings.json)

```
"ApplicationInsights": {
  "InstrumentationKey": "YOUR-INSTRUMENTATION-KEY"
}
```

Use SDK to Track Custom Events

```
telemetryClient.TrackEvent("UserSignedUp", new Dictionary<string,
string> {
    { "Plan", "Pro" }
```

```
});
```

Analyze Logs

Use Log Analytics to run KQL queries:

```
requests
| where success == false
| summarize count() by resultCode
```

Project 7: Deploy a Containerized App Using Azure Container Apps

Overview

Containerize a Node.js app and deploy it to Azure Container Apps with autoscaling based on requests per second.

Services Used

- Azure Container Registry (ACR)

- Azure Container Apps

Dockerfile Sample

```
FROM node:18
WORKDIR /app
COPY . .
RUN npm install
CMD ["node", "index.js"]
```

Deployment Steps

1. Build and push to ACR.

2. Create container app and configure ingress + scaling.

3. Monitor using Azure Monitor metrics.

Project 8: Secure API Access with Azure AD B2C

Overview

Integrate Azure AD B2C into a web application for user authentication using OpenID Connect.

Services Used

- Azure AD B2C

- App Service

- Microsoft.Identity.Web (SDK)

Key Snippet (Startup.cs in .NET app)

```
services.AddAuthentication(OpenIdConnectDefaults.AuthenticationScheme)


.AddMicrosoftIdentityWebApp(Configuration.GetSection("AzureAdB2C"));
```

appsettings.json

```
"AzureAdB2C": {
  "Instance": "https://your-tenant.b2clogin.com",
  "ClientId": "your-client-id",
  "Domain": "your-tenant.onmicrosoft.com",
  "SignUpSignInPolicyId": "B2C_1_SignUpIn"
}
```

Project 9: Deploy a Static Web App with GitHub Integration

Overview

Host a static front-end site (React, Angular, or Vue) on Azure Static Web Apps with GitHub integration.

Services Used

- Azure Static Web Apps

- GitHub Actions

- Azure Functions (optional for backend API)

```
azure-static-web-apps.yml
app_location: "/"
api_location: "api"
output_location: "build"
```

Benefits

- Global CDN

- Custom domains + SSL

- Built-in auth providers (GitHub, Twitter, Azure AD)

Project 10: Create an Azure DevTest Lab Environment

Overview

Create a cost-controlled lab environment for development or testing.

Services Used

- Azure DevTest Labs

- ARM/Bicep templates

- Policy for auto-shutdown

Key Features

- VM provisioning with approved images

- Schedule-based shutdown/startup

- Integrated with Azure Policy for budget enforcement

Best Practices for Project Work

- Use version control (Git/GitHub) for all projects

- Document each project in a README.md file with:

- ○ Overview

- ○ Architecture diagram

- ○ Steps to run/deploy

- ○ Screenshots (if possible)

- Deploy to multiple environments (dev/staging/prod)

- Incorporate CI/CD, security, and monitoring in each project

- Revisit projects to update with newer Azure features or services

Summary

These sample projects are designed to provide a realistic view of working with Azure in various capacities—development, infrastructure, DevOps, security, and data. They not only build your technical proficiency but also serve as excellent portfolio items to showcase to employers or clients.

Key Takeaways:

- Apply theory through guided and custom-built projects

- Use these examples as templates to solve real-world challenges

- Document and share your projects to build credibility

- Continuously refactor and improve projects as Azure evolves

- Emphasize architecture, security, and automation in every build

In the next section, you'll find an **API Reference Guide**, outlining common service APIs and SDK calls you can use to programmatically interact with Azure.

API Reference Guide

Modern cloud development heavily relies on automation and integration. Whether you're building infrastructure-as-code scripts, integrating Azure services with third-party tools, or enabling programmatic access to your applications, Azure APIs and SDKs empower you to control resources with precision. Azure provides multiple interfaces—REST APIs, SDKs in various languages, the Azure CLI, and PowerShell—for interacting with its services.

This section provides an extensive API reference guide, including REST endpoints, SDK methods, and code snippets for key services such as Azure Resource Manager, Storage, App Services, Functions, Key Vault, Cosmos DB, and more. The guide is not exhaustive but is structured to help you get started with the most commonly used operations.

Azure Resource Manager (ARM) API

Azure Resource Manager provides a consistent management layer that enables you to create, update, and delete resources within your Azure subscription.

Base URL:

```
https://management.azure.com/
```

Common Headers:

```
Authorization: Bearer <access_token>
Content-Type: application/json
```

List Resource Groups

```
GET /subscriptions/{subscriptionId}/resourcegroups?api-version=2021-
04-01
```

Create Resource Group (JSON body)

```
{
   "location": "eastus"
}
```

Sample cURL

```
curl -X PUT
https://management.azure.com/subscriptions/<sub_id>/resourcegroups/M
yRG?api-version=2021-04-01 \
-H "Authorization: Bearer <token>" \
-H "Content-Type: application/json" \
-d '{"location": "eastus"}'
```

Azure Storage REST API

Azure Storage offers REST interfaces for Blob, Table, Queue, and File storage.

Blob Upload

```
PUT /mycontainer/myblob HTTP/1.1
Host: myaccount.blob.core.windows.net
x-ms-blob-type: BlockBlob
Authorization: SharedKey <account-name>:<signature>
```

Get Blob Properties

```
HEAD /mycontainer/myblob HTTP/1.1
```

Sample using Azure SDK (Python)

```python
from azure.storage.blob import BlobServiceClient

client = BlobServiceClient.from_connection_string("<conn_string>")
container_client = client.get_container_client("mycontainer")
blob_client = container_client.get_blob_client("myblob.txt")
blob_client.upload_blob(b"Hello Azure!")
```

Azure App Services API

App Services API supports operations like starting, stopping, and deploying web apps.

Start App

```
POST
/subscriptions/{subscriptionId}/resourceGroups/{resourceGroup}/providers/Microsoft.Web/sites/{siteName}/start?api-version=2022-03-01
```

Stop App

```
POST /.../{siteName}/stop?api-version=2022-03-01
```

Deploy Zip Package

```
PUT https://<app-name>.scm.azurewebsites.net/api/zipdeploy
```

Use Kudu API for deployments and diagnostics.

Kudu API Authentication

- Basic Auth using `$username` and `publishingPassword`

- Token-based auth using `SCM_DO_BUILD_DURING_DEPLOYMENT`

Azure Functions API

Functions are triggered by events and expose HTTP endpoints when using HTTP triggers.

Function URL Format:

```
https://<functionapp>.azurewebsites.net/api/<function-
name>?code=<function_key>
```

Sample Payload:

```
{
  "name": "Jane Doe",
  "email": "jane@example.com"
}
```

Sample Function (JavaScript)

```
module.exports = async function (context, req) {
    context.res = {
        status: 200,
        body: { message: `Hello ${req.body.name}` }
    };
}
```

Azure Key Vault API

Used to store and retrieve secrets, certificates, and keys.

Base URL:

```
https://<vault-name>.vault.azure.net
```

Get Secret

```
GET /secrets/{secret-name}?api-version=7.4
```

Create/Update Secret

```
PUT /secrets/{secret-name}?api-version=7.4
{
  "value": "mySuperSecretValue"
}
```

Sample using SDK (Node.js)

```javascript
const { SecretClient } = require("@azure/keyvault-secrets");
const { DefaultAzureCredential } = require("@azure/identity");

const vaultName = "myvault";
const url = `https://${vaultName}.vault.azure.net`;

const client = new SecretClient(url, new DefaultAzureCredential());
await client.setSecret("apiKey", "abc123");
```

Cosmos DB API

Supports multiple APIs: SQL, MongoDB, Cassandra, Gremlin, Table.

SQL API REST Endpoint
```
POST
https://<account>.documents.azure.com/dbs/<db>/colls/<collection>/do
cs
x-ms-documentdb-isquery: true
x-ms-version: 2018-12-31
Authorization: <auth header>
```

Query Document

```json
{
  "query": "SELECT * FROM c WHERE c.name = @name",
  "parameters": [
    { "name": "@name", "value": "Alice" }
```

```
    ]
}
```

Sample SDK (Python)

```python
from azure.cosmos import CosmosClient

client = CosmosClient("<url>", "<key>")
db = client.get_database_client("ProductsDB")
container = db.get_container_client("Items")

item = { "id": "1", "name": "Laptop", "price": 1200 }
container.upsert_item(item)
```

Azure DevOps REST API

Azure DevOps exposes a REST API for managing pipelines, repos, artifacts, and boards.

Base URL:

```
https://dev.azure.com/{organization}/{project}/_apis/
```

List Repositories

```
GET /git/repositories?api-version=7.1-preview.1
```

Trigger Pipeline

```
POST /pipelines/{pipelineId}/runs?api-version=6.0-preview.1
{
  "resources": {
    "repositories": {
      "self": {
        "refName": "refs/heads/main"
      }
    }
  }
}
```

Sample using curl

```
curl -u user:PAT
https://dev.azure.com/org/project/_apis/build/builds?api-version=6.0
```

Azure CLI and SDK Equivalents

Each API operation can be mirrored in Azure CLI or SDKs.

Operation	Azure CLI Example
Create Resource Group	`az group create -n MyRG -l eastus`
Create Web App	`az webapp create --name myapp --plan myplan`
List Blobs	`az storage blob list --account-name mystorage ...`
Create VM	`az vm create --name MyVM --image UbuntuLTS ...`
Key Vault Secret	`az keyvault secret show --name mysecret --vault-name myvault`

Authentication and Tokens

Azure APIs require proper authentication. Options include:

- **Azure AD Tokens** (OAuth2): For user or service principal access

- **Managed Identities**: For apps running in Azure

- **Shared Keys**: For storage and Cosmos DB

- **PAT (Personal Access Token)**: For DevOps

Azure AD Token Example (CLI)

```
az account get-access-token --resource https://management.azure.com/
```

Helpful SDK Repositories

- **.NET**: https://github.com/Azure/azure-sdk-for-net

- **JavaScript/TypeScript**: https://github.com/Azure/azure-sdk-for-js

- **Python**: https://github.com/Azure/azure-sdk-for-python

- **Java**: https://github.com/Azure/azure-sdk-for-java

Tools for Testing APIs

- **Postman**: Import Swagger/OpenAPI specs, test Azure REST endpoints

- **Insomnia**: Lightweight API tester with environment variables

- **Swagger UI**: Azure APIs often expose OpenAPI specs for self-hosting

- **Fiddler / Charles Proxy**: Monitor real-time traffic for debugging

Summary

This API reference guide provides foundational and practical examples for interacting with key Azure services programmatically. Mastering these interfaces enables automation, customization, and scalability for your applications and infrastructure. Whether using REST endpoints or SDKs, integrating Azure programmatically enhances both developer velocity and solution robustness.

Key Takeaways:

- REST APIs provide full control over Azure resources, often used with service principals or automation scripts.

- SDKs simplify development in your preferred language.

- Azure CLI offers quick command-line access and scripting capabilities.

- Combine APIs with CI/CD, automation, and observability for production-grade systems.

- Secure API access using identity platforms like Azure AD and Key Vault.

In the next and final appendix section, we'll cover **Frequently Asked Questions (FAQs)**— answering common queries that developers, architects, and cloud learners encounter on their Azure journey.

Frequently Asked Questions

Over the course of working with Azure—whether as a developer, architect, DevOps engineer, or beginner—there are recurring questions that arise. These questions typically revolve around best practices, platform limits, pricing, deployment strategies, integration scenarios, security, and learning resources. This section aggregates and answers the most frequently asked questions from the community, exam prep, interviews, and real-world projects to provide clarity and practical guidance.

General Questions

Q: What is the difference between Azure Resource Manager (ARM) and the Azure Portal?
A: Azure Resource Manager is the underlying deployment and management service that Azure uses for all resources. Every action taken in the Azure Portal (e.g., creating a VM or storage account) is translated into an ARM API call. The Portal is a GUI frontend, while ARM supports templates and automation for infrastructure-as-code.

Q: Can I use Azure without a credit card?
A: Yes, to some extent. Students can use Azure for Students (https://azure.microsoft.com/free/students/) which provides credits without needing a credit card. Microsoft Learn also offers sandbox environments that do not require a card.

Q: How do I check which Azure services are available in my region?
A: Use the Azure Products by Region page:
https://azure.microsoft.com/en-us/global-infrastructure/services

Or run this command:

```
az account list-locations -o table
```

Billing and Cost

Q: How do I prevent accidental overspending?
A: Use the following methods:

- Set up budgets and alerts in Azure Cost Management.

- Enable auto-shutdown on VMs for dev/test environments.

- Use tags to track resources by project or department.

- Use DevTest Labs for controlled provisioning.

Q: Does the Azure Free Tier expire?
A: Yes and no. Azure offers a **12-month free tier** (with specific services and a $200 credit in the first 30 days), and certain services are **always free** under limited usage (e.g., 750 hours/month of B1S VM).

Q: How can I estimate the cost of my deployment?
A: Use the Azure Pricing Calculator:
https://azure.microsoft.com/en-us/pricing/calculator

Or via CLI:

```
az consumption usage list
```

Identity and Access Management

Q: What is the difference between Azure AD and Active Directory?
A: Azure AD is Microsoft's cloud-based identity and access management service, designed for managing cloud applications. Traditional AD is on-premises and focuses on domain-joined Windows environments. Azure AD does not support LDAP or group policy like traditional AD.

Q: How can I give someone read-only access to my subscription?
A: Assign them the **Reader** role at the subscription or resource group level:

```
az role assignment create \
  --assignee <userPrincipalName> \
  --role Reader \
  --scope /subscriptions/<subscriptionId>
```

Q: What is the purpose of a Managed Identity?
A: Managed Identity allows Azure resources (like VMs or Function Apps) to authenticate with other Azure services (like Key Vault or SQL DB) without needing to store credentials. It uses Azure AD behind the scenes.

Development and Deployment

Q: Should I use ARM, Bicep, or Terraform?
A: Use Bicep if you want a simpler, more readable abstraction of ARM templates and prefer Microsoft-native tooling. Use Terraform for multi-cloud or open-source projects where vendor neutrality and community modules are important.

Q: How can I deploy to Azure directly from GitHub?
A: Use GitHub Actions to automate your CI/CD process. Azure provides official GitHub Actions for:

- Web Apps

- Static Web Apps

- Azure CLI/PowerShell

- Key Vault secret retrieval

Example:

```
- uses: azure/webapps-deploy@v2
  with:
    app-name: 'myapp'
    package: '.'
```

Q: What's the difference between Azure App Service and Azure Functions?
A: Azure App Service is for hosting web applications with persistent infrastructure. Azure Functions is for event-driven, serverless workloads that scale automatically and bill per execution. Use Functions for small isolated tasks; use App Services for full web apps.

Q: How do I rollback a deployment in Azure App Service?
A: App Service supports deployment slots and swap operations. You can maintain a staging slot and swap back if needed. Alternatively, use version control tags and redeploy previous builds via GitHub or Azure DevOps.

Security

Q: How do I securely store secrets in Azure?
A: Use **Azure Key Vault**. Secrets can be referenced by Function Apps, Web Apps, or VMs using managed identity without exposing them in source code.

Example:

```
az keyvault secret set --name dbPassword --value "supersecret123" --
vault-name MyVault
```

Q: What is Azure Defender for Cloud?
A: Defender for Cloud is Azure's threat protection and security posture management tool. It provides security assessments, recommendations, compliance tracking, and alerts for cloud workloads (including AWS and GCP via connectors).

Q: How can I enforce secure resource configurations?
A: Use **Azure Policy** to define rules like "Only use approved VM sizes" or "All storage accounts must have encryption enabled." You can audit or enforce policies at the subscription or management group level.

Networking

Q: What is the difference between a Virtual Network and a Subnet?
A: A Virtual Network (VNet) is the overall isolated network within Azure. Subnets are subdivisions within the VNet that help organize resources and apply network security policies.

Q: How do I access a private Azure SQL Database from my local machine?
A: Use **Private Endpoint** or **VPN Gateway** to create a secure connection. You can also allow your IP in the SQL firewall settings temporarily.

Q: What is Azure Front Door vs. Traffic Manager?
A: Azure Front Door is a global application delivery network with SSL termination, WAF, and URL routing. Traffic Manager is a DNS-based load balancer for distributing traffic across regions or endpoints based on priority, geography, or latency.

Monitoring and Troubleshooting

Q: How do I troubleshoot application issues in Azure?
A: Use:

- **Application Insights**: For application-level logging and tracing.

- **Azure Monitor**: For infrastructure metrics and logs.

- **Log Analytics (KQL)**: For custom queries across collected data.

- **Alerts and Workbooks**: For visualizations and proactive notification.

Q: Can I view detailed logs of my Azure Functions?
A: Yes, by enabling Application Insights. Logs can be queried using Kusto Query Language (KQL):

```
traces
| where message contains "Error"
| project timestamp, message
```

Q: What are some best practices for alerting?
A:

- Set alerts on high CPU/memory usage

- Monitor failed deployments or login attempts

- Integrate alerts with Microsoft Teams, Slack, or PagerDuty

- Use Action Groups to define notification and remediation steps

Certification and Learning

Q: Which certification should I start with?
A: AZ-900 (Azure Fundamentals) is a great starting point. It covers core concepts and is suitable even for non-technical roles. From there, follow the path that aligns with your goals (e.g., AZ-204 for developers, AZ-104 for administrators).

Q: How often do Microsoft certifications expire?
A: Most certifications require renewal **annually**, which can be done online for free. Microsoft sends reminders and offers renewal assessments on Microsoft Learn.

Q: Are sandbox environments free?
A: Yes. Microsoft Learn provides temporary sandboxes for hands-on training that do not affect your personal subscription or billing.

Miscellaneous

Q: Can I automate everything in Azure?
A: Practically yes. You can automate deployments, scaling, monitoring, networking, and even security configurations using a mix of:

- Azure CLI / PowerShell

- REST APIs

- SDKs

- ARM / Bicep / Terraform

- GitHub Actions / Azure DevOps Pipelines

Q: How can I stay up to date with Azure?
A:

- Subscribe to Azure Updates

- Follow @Azure, @MarkRussinovich on X (formerly Twitter)

- Watch Azure Friday and Ignite/Build recordings

- Read the Azure Monthly newsletter

Summary

This FAQ section is designed to address the practical challenges and common concerns you'll face when working with Azure. The answers are drawn from community wisdom, Microsoft documentation, and real-world usage. Refer back here as needed and continue asking questions—curiosity is a key asset in cloud development.

Key Takeaways:

- Use Azure Policy, Key Vault, and RBAC for secure, compliant deployments

- Lean on App Services, Functions, and DevOps tools for scalable delivery

- Embrace learning resources like Microsoft Learn and GitHub Actions

- Use logs, alerts, and telemetry to maintain visibility into your systems

- Community forums, certifications, and hands-on practice are your allies

This concludes the appendices and the full contents of *Azure 101: The No-Fluff Beginner's Guide*. Stay curious, stay hands-on, and continue building great things in the cloud.

302 | Code On The Cloud

www.ingramcontent.com/pod-product-compliance
Lightning Source LLC
LaVergne TN
LVHW051434050326
832903LV00030BD/3077